CW00347549

the dream

LEIGH LAWSON

the dream

An Actor's Story

OBERON BOOKS
LONDON

First published in 2008 by Oberon Books Ltd
521 Caledonian Road, London N7 9RH
tel 020 7607 3637 / fax 020 7607 3629
info@oberonbooks.com / www.oberonbooks.com

Text copyright © Leigh Lawson 2008

"My Blue Heaven" copyright © George Whiting and Walter Donaldson, reproduced by permission of EMI Music Ltd and Memory Lane Ltd

"You Were There" copyright © Estate of Noël Coward, reproduced by permission of Alan Brodie Representation Ltd

Leigh Lawson is hereby identified as author of this work in accordance with section 77 of the Copyright, Designs and Patents Act 1988. All rights reserved.

This book is sold subject to the condition that it shall not by way of trade or otherwise be circulated without the publisher's consent in any form of binding or cover, stored in a retrieval system or circulated electronically, other than that in which it is published and without a similar condition including this condition being imposed on any subsequent purchaser.

A catalogue record for this book is available from the British Library.

Cover illustration by Andrzej Klimowski

ISBN: 978-1-84002-867-6

Printed in Great Britain by CPI Antony Rowe, Chippenham

For those I love, and who love me.
You know who you are.

Contents

Introduction

If the curtains are open at a window, I can't resist standing outside and gaping in. Stopping to gaze through a window as I pass has since being a child become not so much a curiosity, more a compulsion. Especially at night when curtains are left open and the scene is lit like a movie.

I sit at pavement café tables and watch people go by, noting how they walk, how they dress, how they speak. I make up stories, who they are, what their relationship is. I pretend to read a book, but really I'm listening to the people talking at the next table. Under any other circumstances, I might have been taken into care, put on medication. But because I'm not an obvious threat to society, I have managed to avoid arrest and make my living as an actor.

Actors are not normal. It's a weird path to choose to tread. These are the primary reasons I'm convinced I made the right career choice forty years ago.

I'd more or less enjoyed thirty of those forty years, working pretty well consistently in film, TV and theatre, when I was asked to play Loveless in *The Relapse* at the Royal Shakespeare Company. This was to be my first appearance at the RSC. Albeit when I graduated from RADA in 1969, I was offered a one-line spear-carrying part by the RSC casting department. But I had declined the not very tempting offer, and went instead into three-weekly repertory theatre – the attraction being a variety of leading roles and character parts. Perhaps carrying a spear, and trying to discover a way of saying –

"He approacheth e'en as we speak, my lord"

– in a way after four hundred years never discovered by an actor before, might have lead to wielding a sword at Elsinore or Agincourt.

But then again, maybe not.

Ten years or so ago, during *The Relapse* and *A Midsummer Night's Dream*, I for some reason, felt the necessity to keep a record of my strange compulsions. I then put it away in a drawer of my desk and there it languished for the best part of ten years. Now I find it's to be published.

It's weird being an actor.

I owe many thanks to the following:

The magical Caroline Michel for making my life wonderfully weirder. The unflaggingly erudite support of James Hogan. The invaluable help and guidance of my editor Stephen Watson. Charles Glanville, James Stephens, Daisy Bowie-Sell, Margaret Byron, Jo Dyer and all at Oberon Books for allowing a fledgling writer to flutter his literary wings in the safe nest of Caledonian Road. Bruce Robinson, for his encouragement. The brilliance of Andrzej Klimowski for my dream book cover, and a special thanks to the wondrous Lindy King who's always there for me however the dice fall.

Leigh Lawson
October 2008

Acknowledgements

Leigh Lawson and Oberon Books would like to thank the following photographers for permission to use their photographs: Brian Aris, Alan Markfield, Clive Barda, Donald Cooper.

Every effort has been made to track down other photographers whose work is included in the plate section.

London

ONE

"What's past is prologue"
William Shakespeare

"How true is that philosophy which says
  Our heaven is seated in our minds!
  Through all the roving pleasures of my youth,
  Where nights and days seemed all consumed in joy,
  Where the false face of luxury
  Displayed such charms
  As might have shaken the most holy hermit
  And made him totter at his altar,
  I never knew one moment's peace like this.
  Here, in this little soft retreat,
  My thoughts unbent from all the cares of life,
  Content with fortune,
  Eased from the grating duties of dependence,
  From envy flee, ambition underfoot,
  The raging flame of wild destructive lust
  Reduced to a warm pleasing fire of lawful love,
  My life glides on, and all is well within."

The lines keep running through my brain.

It's dark but a little light seeps through a crack in the velvet curtains. I'm lying in bed, Kate lies beside me. I wear a long muslin shirt, she a simple white cotton shift. We link little fingers and tug as has become our custom before we do it. Kate dives under the bed covers.

Oh God.

A red light flashes.

The curtains part and we're pushed from the twilight of the wings onto the brightly-lit stage. I address the audience.

"How true is that philosophy which says
  Our heaven is seated in our minds..."

The opening lines of my penultimate performance as Loveless in *The Relapse* by Vanbrugh.

In the interval almost the entire company meet backstage for a smoke in the long corridor that serves our dressing rooms. To cater for a minority there is a "no smoking in the dressing room" policy at the Barbican Theatre, London home of the Royal Shakespeare Company.

The innovative talents of the architect responsible for the alienating building led him also to the inspired concept of putting the Green Room several floors below the dressing rooms. Consequently very few of the actors have either the time, or inclination, to make the four-flight trek there and back during the fifteen-minute intermission. As a result the dressing room corridor resembles a scene from a Fellini movie: actors milling around in a centuries-spanning eclectic collection of costumes, from the Elizabethan-clad *The Taming of the Shrew* company appearing in the main theatre, to us in the Pit Theatre in Restoration garb. Cigarette smoke and a humorous comforting camaraderie pervade the concrete corridor. A feeling of continuity. I'm going to miss it.

> "Content with fortune...
> From envy flee, ambition underfoot."

Dressing rooms are shared in the Pit Theatre; I share with four other actors. Before this production I hadn't shared a dressing room for many years. I'm not at all surprised to rediscover how much I enjoy the arrangement.

There is one single bunk-type bed in our dressing room, but like an appealing chair at the fireside of an old country pub, you feel instinctively that this is someone else's territory. The someone in this case is the senior member of our cast, Victor Spinetti. Victor could not be mistaken for anything other than an actor. He resides behind a curtained partition separating him from the rest of us, and from there he regales us all constantly with theatrical stories and anecdotes. His repertoire is vast and unending, told with great relish and panache, and more often than not has a homosexual theme. I recognised from day one this is a man of the theatre-theatre. A cult figure in the 1960s, he appeared in the Beatles films *A Hard Day's Night* and *Help!* and directed the musical *Hair* on stage and some John Lennon work at the Old Vic. He sometimes, if we're alone in the dressing room, comes to sit in my section and relates stories of when he was butch and heterosexual, living with a rich widow.

He has a big kindness about him – but then in my considerable experience 99.5 per cent of people in the theatre have. Contrary to popular belief, it's almost a prerequisite and generally comes with the territory, particularly in this company – whether the territory is on stage, backstage, in the casting department, design department, hair and wigs, every burrow that makes up this theatre warren. It would seem we all want to be happy bunnies.

Victor says the clue to playing his part of Lord Foppington is – "To walk as if walking on eggshells...his expression that of someone with a bad smell under his nose."

This he does to his, and the audience's, outrageous delight at every performance.

He has a Welsh accent at times backstage, which strikes me as slightly incongruous for someone whose surname is Spinetti.

Anyway, as sure as the fireside chair in the pub belongs to the old farmer, so it is in our dressing room for the one bunk bed, and the rest of us put our feet up on a chair, a folded towel under our heads on the floor, to rest and recharge our batteries for the evening performance. Sometimes, earplugs are an added useful device for the duel purpose of resting undisturbed through other thesps' snores and farts, and the over-enthusiastic endeavours of the trumpet-playing student just across the alley from our window at the Royal College of Music. A more musical matching of farts and snores could not be imagined. It's not too uncomfortable but I suppose could be construed as undignified.

I love it.

The other actors sharing the one-bed dormitory are Christopher Godwin, tall, very thin, about 50 years old. He makes me laugh a lot and, I get the impression, is – or was – something of a rebel. He has an old, yellowing letter in a small frame that rests against his dressing table mirror recording his first rejection after drama school, from the director of a seaside repertory company. It reads something like:

> "Although enjoying your audition, it was not possible to offer you a place in this company on account of us having a very low budget and you being so tall it makes our scenery look small. We do not have the financial resources to rectify this problem."

I imagine the only Christmas panto the company could ever do would be *Snow White and the Seven Dwarfs*.

There's a story going around the company at the moment about one particularly disliked, spiky director who was recently directing a show that included some dwarfs. When his assistant director informed him at rehearsal that the poor little sod that had been asked to do a somersault across the stage, couldn't do it, the director in a very loud voice, yelled: "Well, what's the point of being a dwarf if you can't do a fucking somersault?"

Chris does the most intricate make-up each performance for his part as Old Coupler: a masterful technique of shading and colour. A myriad of tiny criss-crossed lines transform his bony face into a pox-ridden skull. I bitterly regret not sitting with him at his mirror and learning how to do it – how very stupid of me; I'll probably never get the chance again.

For his role in the play Christopher wears a very generous false phallus and testicles filled with dried lentils under his knickerbocker trousers which he, his dresser, and the audience, enjoy very much indeed.

I always go down early for my second entrance to watch him on stage from the wings. He is brave, funny and cheeky;

from his first scene I can judge the comedic temperature of the audience.

Michael Gardiner is playing Worthy. Early forties, handsome with thinning brown hair. He spends a lot of his time offstage painstakingly painting tiny miniature figures of fantastical warriors for his children to play games with. He also understudies Victor and was "on" for a week when Victor was ill; he was also a brilliant Lord Foppington, not in the least imitative of Victor – he pursued his own quite different vision.

Christopher Benjamin, playing Sir Tunbelly Clumsy, sits next to me at the dressing table. In his early sixties, a large man with a large nose, and a large stomach, he arrives each day on a large motorbike. He loves his large motorbike. He also loves watching or listening to cricket, football and motor-racing – in fact, I think most sports. When he came on stage just before the end of the play recently, I knew England had won the soccer game he had been listening to on his Walkman in the dressing room because of the renewed energy and excitement in his performance. Soon he was giving secret little signals and signs to other interested members of the cast who received them with a surreptitious nod or smile.

This was by no means the first, or to be the last, covert inter-cast communication on stage. Before this afternoon's matinee performance Lionel Guyett, who plays the demented Doctor Syringe, suggested for the matinee performance that each member of the cast has to mention a fish during the play, but the rules dictate no one can mention the same fish twice. A challenge.

The proposed game offered excitement and danger, because of course the audience must never know, or for that matter the stage manager, or for that matter the director or assistant director who may be watching, the consequence for which could be a severe bollocking after the show.

Being in a Restoration play is a bit of gift for such a game. To a good percentage of the audience, and some of the actors, certain passages are pretty incomprehensible anyway.

Playing the roguish Loveless presented me with a fine opportunity so, with no other takers in the cast, in my second scene instead of "Thou art a veritable coxswain" I kick off with:

"Thou art a veritable codpiece."

Simple. Dead easy.

If the director brings this up – I can easily excuse it as an actor's slip of the mind.

But the astonished look of delight on the face of Lionel Guyett came dangerously close to giving the game away – not helped by his then inability to deliver with the necessary gravitas the tirade of abuse that was supposed to follow. Uncontrollable gasps and giggles ensued to the point where he could hardly speak, or even splutter. The rest of the cast turned upstage and all I could see were rows of convulsively shaking shoulders, no one daring to look another in the eye.

The die is cast, the gauntlet down, the challenge irrefutably made. Who would now dare not to go a-fishmongering?

"Lady Kipper awaits in her carriage, Madame" – a brave one.

"You young sprat" – very period.

"A whale of a time" – not technically a fish but, after some debate backstage, appreciably received.

"She's naught but an old trout" – perfection.

The following acts are littered with mackerel, sole, hake, sardines, prawns, cockles, mussels, crabs, winkles, sharks and eel.

As we take our curtain call I can almost hear a cheer from the cast and see fists punching the air as we all silently scream, "Yes, we've done it".

We're home and dry. Or hung and dried.

Back in the dressing room, the usual hyper-charged atmosphere after the show. Adrenaline rush.

The dual satisfaction of a job well done laced with a cobweb of sadness – the final one to come.

Half an hour before the evening performance, the over-anxious, over-burdened, under-paid assistant director enters our one-bed dorm and does his best I-am-practising-to-be-a-director impersonation –

"Very good show this afternoon, alive and vital, but I don't want to hear any mention of fish in this evening's performance."

Rumbled.

"Don't worry," says a voice that seems to be mine.

"It's vegetables tonight."

So, I am sad to be saying goodbye to all this "fab", "triff" and "brill" good work, good people, good fun. I'd come home. Where else could I find all this?

In New York, that's where.

I ring the Missus as usual between shows.

"Hello, my darling. How was the matinee?" she asks.

"Fine," I say. "But feeling sad – last one coming up."

"Yes, you must be. But listen. I've just had a call from Tony Walton in New York. He's directing Noël Coward's last work, two one-act plays called *Noël Coward In Two Keys* at the Bay Street Theatre, Long Island, New York. Three weeks' rehearsal, three-week limited run. He asked if you would consider playing the lead part? Tim Curry has turned it down last minute, apparently. Start rehearsals in a week's time in New York."

I love Tim Curry as a person, as an actor too. This helps, but, first choice or second must not get in the way on such occasions. Why they didn't have the good sense to come to you in the first place is something every actor has found a valid excuse for when a part he wants to play comes along. Pride must not come into the equation. First choice, second or tenth, it matters not, it matters not a jot. The opportunity to get your teeth into a good part? Now, that matters a lot.

Of course, being first choice is always far better.

"You'll find a copy in the Noël Coward section in the book-shelves," I say, "can you get one over to me?"

"I know, I've found it, it's on its way."

Bless her. What a wife.

No feet on chair, no towel under head for me.

The two Christophers are in the one-bed dorm, reading the new Edward Bond play to be directed by Bond next season; they have interviews with the author next week. A pang of envy. A chance to stay with the company.

"What's it like?" I ask Chris.

"Dunno," says Chris. "Can't understand a word of it – can you Chris?"

"Not a fucking word, Chris," says Chris to Chris.

I read the first of my entirely comprehensible plays, a bit frothy and superficial, playing a southern American stereotype business tycoon called Vernon, light and inconsequential, a curtain raiser. Second play brilliant. An Englishman, a writer called Sir Hugo. The dark side of Coward dealing with his homosexuality. A cleverly written and constructed one-act drama. The plays are two separate one-act pieces that take place in the same hotel suite in Switzerland. Coward was to comment in his diaries on seeing Neil Simon's *Plaza Suite* – written several years later – "I wonder where he got *that* idea from?"

Some of the depression of saying goodbye to the company is numbed by the triple Prozac effect of – new script – new job – New York.

An end of run party in rehearsal room No 2. Not a suitable place for a party ever, and inevitably an anti-climax. Too much past emotion soaked into those black walls to accommodate a relaxed, off-guard party atmosphere. Whatever the DJ plays, the music belongs somewhere else. And now so do we; the conversation is forced and unnatural but perhaps any venue would be unsuitable when people don't really want to say goodbye. But know they must.

Tony Walton rings to ask would I like to do *Noël Coward In Two Keys*?

"Are you joking, Tony? I'd pay to do it."

Which turns out to be rather prophetic. Bay Street is a small theatre in a small town called Sag Harbor on Long Island, New York, and the salary reflects the proportions of the theatre and town, i.e. small.

Finishing *The Relapse*, saying goodbye to the company has left a void in my life. At 7.30 pm I don't want to sit down to dinner: I want to be at the theatre with my friends in the one-bed dorm, donning my white muslin shirt, lying in bed with Kate – going on stage, playing Loveless. But the spirit of the play is what bound us together. That spirit has flown. Five more days and so have I.

New York

TWO

The first week of rehearsals are to be held here in New York City: the gods look down, give us a nod and a wink, and arrange for my wife to be recording the final tracks of her new album in New York the very week I'm rehearsing there. We're grateful for their attention to detail.

My wife's name is Lesley. Her professional name is Twiggy. Most people that know her call her Twiggs. It's confusing. I tend to fluctuate between all three, with splatterings of Darling, Angel and Gorgeous.

We're staying with Tony Walton and his wife Gen LeRoy in their huge apartment on Broadway on the Upper West Side of Manhattan. We usually stay with them in New York. Tony and Gen are like family. I can truly say I love these two people.

Tony is British but at the end of his first marriage to Julie Andrews over thirty years ago, he found himself in America, and stayed. Four years ago, after a try-out period of twenty-five years, Tony and Gen decided to get married. Tony is not an impulsive person.

For his theatre design he has so many Tony Awards and nominations they could have been named after him, a handful of Academy Award nominations, an Oscar for his work in film, and just about every other accolade and recognition of his brilliant work. He is a gentle soul and one of the most generous of spirit and kindest people on the planet. *Noël Coward In Two Keys* is to be Tony's directing debut.

Gen is an Italian-American and seems to have sifted everything that's good about both cultures and made them her own. She's a gifted writer for stage and screen. The American artist Norman Rockwell used Gen as a model when she was younger and her pretty face can easily be recognised in some of his paintings and illustrations.

Rehearsals are held in an old warren of a building, downtown on 3rd Street, but things have been so beautifully arranged from above, that at the end of a day's rehearsals I can walk uptown a few blocks to the studio where Twiggs is recording her new album *London Pride*, and sneak in to listen with tears in my eyes and a heart bursting with pride for my ever so talented girl singing songs from British musicals.

*

> "Courage is being scared to death
> and saddling up anyway."
>
> *John Wayne*

I walk into the rehearsal room on the first day to see rows of about forty chairs stretching back from the front of the long table that the cast will eventually sit behind to read the play out loud for the first time. Around the table sit the other members of the cast.

Bebe Neuwirth – small, with curly black hair framing a pretty face. Guardedly friendly. When she smiles her even lips reveal perfect white teeth and you want her to smile always. Already making her name on Broadway in musicals, this is her first straight play.

"Are you nervous?" I ask, desperate for someone to share my fear with.

"No," she replies convincingly, "should I be?"

My bowels almost collapse.

Dee Hoty is from Texas, I'm told. Tall and striking. The sculpted face and figure of a dancer, a free infectious laugh, and mind as fast as a bullet from a ranger's gun. Both she and Bebe are highly thought of Broadway musical performers. This is also her first straight play.

Bobby Cannavale is playing the waiter. Early twenties, dark swarthy complexion, half Cuban, half Italian, very talented

I'm told; the son-in-law of the film and theatre director Sidney Lumet.

I look around as the rows of chairs fill up. Through the unfocused blur of fear, I recognise only two people sitting on the front row: Sybil Burton, Richard's first wife; and Emma Walton, Tony's daughter from his marriage to Julie Andrews. Together Sybil and Emma run the Bay Street Theatre.

But who are all these other people? And why doesn't someone ask them to leave?

We're about to start the read-through. I'm the only Britisher in the cast and in the first play I'm playing an American. I'm about to make a complete toss-pot of myself and I'd like to do it in front of as few people as possible please.

Am I mad? What could I have been thinking of when I agreed to do this? I want to run back to London and be in an Edward Bond play that nobody understands.

I try to console myself by telling me I must be brave and dangerous. What are they going to do? They can't shoot me for a bad reading. The worst that can happen is that I am told they made a terrible mistake, the two parts are obviously beyond me, and they have to re-cast. As this little comfort-giver passes through my addled brain, I realise I'd rather be shot.

The reading is like dragging my body through a thick slimy swamp. And there are alligators gathered around the swamp. Forty of 'em. All sitting on wooden chairs looking at me, and smiling. Dee is doing brilliantly with her English accent: a few little things but nothing that can't be fixed. Bobby has more charms than a bracelet but hasn't quite decided whether he's British or Swiss. Bebe is doing a subtle, perfectly judged, incredibly accurate German accent. Me? I'm in a swamp in South Carolina with alligators staring at me.

We finish.

"Thank you, that was thrilling," says director Tony.

"Wonderful Texas accent Leigh," says Sybil from the banks of the swamp, but what does she know? She's Welsh.

Who cares? I'm grateful. Any Port Talbot in a storm.

I recently read a biography about Syb's first husband, the actor Richard Burton. In the book it says that whatever research the biographer did, whoever he spoke to, he could find no one with a single bad word to say about Sybil. Though *she* had plenty to complain about. You'd have to be demented not to love her. She's as warm as a fireside on a wet Sunday in the Welsh Valleys. Straightforward but kind, with an encyclopaedic knowledge of the drama.

Emma Walton is about half a lifetime younger than Sybil: blonde, pretty, enigmatic, charming and shy, and equally dedicated to the Bay Street Theatre. Together they have put Bay Street on the theatrical map, attracting many Broadway actors, performers, writers and directors.

Friday night we leave New York for two weeks more rehearsal at the Bay Street Theatre, Sag Harbour, Long Island. Tony and Gen are jeeping it to their house in Sag Harbor. Bebe and Dee are driving up together in Bebe's car to stay at the Barons Cove Motel.

Bobby Cannavale and me, having aspirations beyond our station, hire a stretch limo with chauffeur to drive us up. What the hell? You're only old once. Bobby to take up residence at the Lumet in-laws' residence in the Hamptons, about fifteen minutes from Sag. I'm staying at the Waltons' des. res. in Sag Harbor.

"I can get a deal on a limo," Bobby says, "ya wanna split it?"

"Yeah, sure, why not?" say I in my best NY-UK way.

"Normally a one and a half hour journey, it takes two and half on a Friday night on account of the tailbacks. All New York heads out for Long Island on Friday Night. Maybe bring sumin' t' eat. Too late to eat when we get there," Bobby advises.

We haven't bonded yet. Cuban-New York-Italian. Scottish-London-Warwickshire lad. And over two decades separating us. But we will.

8 pm. The stretch limo arrives to pick me up with Bobby, Harry the chauffeur, and Bobby's two huge, over-excited, over-friendly Walt Disney ragged mongrel dogs.

I've lived in smaller rooms than this car, and certainly ones less well equipped. There's a radio, tape cassette player, CD system, a small bar with decanters of brandy and whisky, two pull-out veneer tables, a television, a phone for calls out, an intercom through to Harry for use when the glass partition is closed. An acre of fluffy royal-blue carpet stretches between two velvet powder-blue chaise-longue seats at each end of the penthouse interior, and smoked glass windows so we can see out but our adoring fans can't see in.

*

"When whippoorwills call
And evenin' is nigh
I'm happy in my
Blue heaven.
A turn to the left,
A turn to the right,
I'm happy in my
Blue heaven."

George Whiting, "My Blue
Heaven"

We have sushi, fried chicken, fresh sourdough baguettes, a selection of cheeses, salads, fruit, and several bottles of excellent Californian Shiraz. We laugh the entire way. It takes three and a half hours to get to Sag Harbor on account of Harry got lost a coupla times. Bobby and me? We couldn't care less. We're in the blue velvet time capsule. The whole journey seemed like fifteen minutes to my new buddy, Bobby, and me.

Sag Harbor, 11.30 pm. I tumble out of blue velvet heaven into my favourite house in the world. Tony and Gen greet me on their porch, we hug. There's a large willow tree in the garden. I put my arms around its trunk and give it a hug. I was married under this tree. It's good to hug trees.

Tony and Gen always have a house full of people staying with them in their rambling old clapboard-clad ex-sea captain's house. Among others, our mutual friend Julie Christie is a guest this weekend. Julie and Harriet Walter were my leading ladies in Pinter's play *Old Times* last year in London's West End, and then Moscow. I give Julie a hug. It's good to hug Julie.

*

> "That inward eye which is the bliss
> of solitude."
>
> *William Wordsworth*

I'm a little concerned I'll not find the solitude I know I like to work in here. I tend to withdraw at this stage of rehearsals. I prefer to spend time in my room alone, have lunch and dinner alone. Pangs of guilt I'm being a bad guest – but there's nothing to be done. This is what I have to do.

I walk alone each day to and from rehearsals along the narrow sidewalk, down the tree-lined lane that leads to the one main street and the silver-grey Atlantic Ocean.

Sag Harbor is an old whaling town that doesn't appear to have changed in over 200 years. Some of the older houses have a flat terraced section of the roof called a "widow's walk" where, in the old days, wives would stand sentry looking out to sea in the hope that their loved ones were returning safely from their perilous Moby Dick adventures.

On the edge of the harbour is the converted Second World War torpedo factory that is now, due to the extraordinary vision of Sybil and Emma, our 350-seat theatre. At night I light my way home with a small flashlight past the tourist shops, the American Hotel, and the eighteenth-century wooden whalers' church where the unlucky widows would pray for the souls of their loved ones lost at sea – dark, empty, silent now. I don't have a car. I don't want one. I ain't goin' nowhere.

A mug of tea. The first cigarette of the day.

Gen shouts up the stairs:

"Phone call for you Leigh. I'll leave the phone outside your door."

It's Michael Foster, my agent in London. A formidable reputation amongst producers and casting directors – adored by his clients. A perfunctory greeting, then characteristically straight to the point.

"The RSC have invited you back to play Oberon and Theseus in *A Midsummer Night's Dream*. Adrian Noble's directing. He's reviving his production with a completely new cast. Are you interested?"

"Am I interested? Does the Pope have a balcony?"

"But there may be a problem."

"What is it?"

"After playing London and Stratford there's a UK tour, followed by a tour of the Far East, then Australia and New Zealand."

"That's a problem?"

"Isn't it?"

"No I don't think so."

"Okay. Well maybe this will be. They start rehearsals, in London, a week before you finish the play you're doing now, in New York."

"Oh Christ, I don't suppose they will but could you ask them if they will wait for me? – Plead?"

"I'll do what I can. Everything okay?"

"Yeah. Fine. I'm tired but I'm okay."

"Take care. Speak to you soon."

I want more than anything to return to the RSC. I want to play Oberon. I want to work with Adrian Noble, the artistic director of the RSC. A sod to miss the chance for the sake of a week. But it's happened before, it will happen again. I don't hold out much hope. If it's meant to happen it will, if not, not. I'm flattered they've asked but I'm aware it's a lot to request a change to their schedule to wait a week for me, it's a long shot. Can't brood over it now. I've got my plate full with Hugo and Vernon.

I walk to rehearsals with Mick Jagger's song "You Can't Always Get What You Want" buzzing around my brain.

All the same, I'd love to play Oberon.

THREE

I still worry about the first of the two plays, *Come into the Garden Maud* in which I play Vernon, the American business-man who goes off the rails. I didn't really like it, completely trust it, when I first read it: although very humorous, surely too light and inconsequential?

I'm told by Dee Hoty my Texan drawl is now perfect.

My other concern focuses on finding the very English Sir Hugo in the second play, *Song at Twilight*. He's intimidating to approach. He's witty and funny, and deadly. How far dare I go? How far do I need to go? How do I get inside and let him take over? I feel like an unwelcome visitor. I sometimes get a glimpse of him through a window but when I try to enter the house, he slams the door in my face.

Don't panic. Don't panic. It'll come. It'll come. But what if this time it doesn't? Can't bash my way in, he'll run away for sure.

Little by little, gently gently, catchy monkey.

No call from Michael Foster re *A Midsummer Night's Dream*. No news is bad news, I suspect. A bowl of dream gone sour.

Spend the day alone in my room. The disciplined slog of learn-ing the words, the worst part of being a working actor. Someone once told me:

"The best part of being an actor is the day they offer you the job, from then on it's a fucking nightmare."

I'm discovering one has to be very precise with Coward, be absolutely on top of the lines. It's written with great economy and precision. Why do I get flashes of Pinter when working on Coward? There's a poetry and a rhythm in Coward's lines that isn't always immediately obvious. It's a voyage of discov-ery. There are ocean depths of emotion running through and between his words.

This second play, *Song at Twilight*, is the darker side of Coward, certainly for most not what one would expect from him. There's definitely some genius at work in here. I remember Christopher Godwin's advice in the one-bed dorm, when was it? Two? Three weeks ago? Seems like an aeon. Did I ever actually have another life before this?

Chris said –

"You have to play Coward on the line. Think it on the line."

Invaluable advice.

Beginning to like the first piece *Come into the Garden Maud* a lot after all, it's fun to play.

Gen shouts up the stairs.

"Phone call from London for you Leigh. I'll leave the phone outside your door."

It's Michael Foster.

"The RSC will wait a week for you. The cast will start rehearsal, you join them a week later when you finish in Sag Harbor."

I want to smother my agent with kisses. Shower him with flowers, presents, give him commission. I love my agent. I love his wife. I love his ex-wife. I love his children. I love his dog.

"Now let me give you the dates."

I deliriously scratch down some of the dates on the back of an old envelope. London, Stratford, Newcastle, Cardiff, Edinburgh, Bath, Plymouth, four and a half weeks off over Christmas, then Japan, Hong Kong, Australia, New Zealand. He then informs me:

"By the by, they've asked if you could have learned the lines of both parts, Theseus and Oberon, before rehearsals commence in London. As time is short you'll only have three and a half weeks' rehearsal by way of missing the first week."

A daunting task but I promise to try.

I can't concentrate on the details of the dates just now. All I need to know is I'm playing Oberon and Theseus back at the

RSC, and when I start. I'll put it away in a little brain box and close the lid till I'm ready to open it. At the moment I need to think about how to make friends with Vernon and Sir Hugo.

I ring Twiggs in London to tell her the news.

"I've been offered Oberon and Theseus in *A Midsummer Nights Dream* at the RSC!"

"Who's directing?"

"Adrian Noble."

"That's wonderful. You'll be brilliant."

"There's a problem. Well, two actually. There's a UK tour, and a tour abroad involved."

"Where?"

"Can't remember exactly, but I think it's Japan, Bangkok or Hong Kong, Australia and I think he said New Zealand."

"Didn't you write it down?"

"I did, but it's all a bit jumbled up on the back of an envelope, but we're only abroad for four and a half weeks."

"How can you do all those countries in four and a half weeks?"

"I don't know darling, they're all close together aren't they?" I say tetchily. I'm getting a bit impatient. Why is she so concerned with the minutiae? – I've been offered Oberon and Theseus at the RSC.

"What's the other problem? You said there were two?"

"I have to start rehearsals as soon as I finish here."

The sound of silence thunders down the phone.

"Hello, are you there?"

"What about our holiday in Bermuda?"

"I won't be able to come."

She reminds me that we've rented the house in Bermuda for a month. It's supposed to be a family holiday.

Guilt kicks in. That most manipulative, unproductive and misleading of emotions.

"I know, I am sorry. Shall I turn the part down?"

"No of course you must do it, I'm thrilled for you but I worry about you, you need a holiday. You haven't had one for three years and I don't enjoy it as much when you're not there."

"I know, I am sorry."

"Never mind, it's not your fault and I'm thrilled for you. I'll ring you tomorrow with details of our arrival. I love you."

"I love you too."

Click.

What is it about long-distance phone calls? That final click.

We had our first preview tonight. I don't remember anything of the performance specifically, the usual blurring white light of fear pervades my brain until the play takes over. Very well received by the audience.

Joy of joys, Twiggs and our son and daughter Ace and Carly have arrived. Although bursting at its clapboard seams with people, Tony and Gen have insisted we stay with them – and we're in heaven. That feeling of deep contentment I get when we are all together again under the same roof. Around the same table. At dinner after the show, some useful observations from Ace concerning the performance. Ace is studying English and Drama at University. He has an instinct, perception, and understanding of theatre beyond his years. He knows my work and I trust his judgement. Always kindly and gently done, he draws my attention to clarity and detail. Twiggs and Carly as always loving and supportive, some useful notes too.

I once read:

"You can only accept criticism when it comes from love; if it comes from any other direction, it's the wrong direction."

After two days of previews, I'm now enjoying the first play. It's great fun and the audience love it. Spend the interval ageing-up for Sir Hugo, grey moustache, grey wig, some age lines and shadows. Just have time before curtain up on Act Two. Can't wait to get back on.

38

Hugo is an embittered old queen based in part on Somerset Maugham and Max Beerbohm and, although he denied it, I'm sure on Coward himself. I know Hugo now and he trusts me. Audible gasps from the audience at times as the veneer is peeled away and the man beneath is revealed.

Bebe, Dee and Bobby are magnificent. We laugh a lot backstage. I think we're going to be okay.

Our crew are the best money can't buy, led by a somewhat eccentric stage manager, Denise Yaney, who sticks little shiny stars in our scripts as prizes if we've done well that day.

The opening night is a Saturday. Strange? No. Clever. Virtually the whole of the influential New York theatre community spend their weekends in the Hamptons, fifteen minutes from here. A lot of them support the Bay Street Theatre.

If I'm honest I don't generally enjoy First Nights as an actor. They're an ordeal to get through. They're – well, they're First Nights.

But tonight's was a different experience. We were on a roll, there was relaxation and trust on stage. It let the audience in, but we were doing it for us, for us, for them.

July 21st – it's my birthday. I've spent the last year thinking I was 53. Twiggs tells me I'm 51. I feel 28. Confusing. I can't think of a better way to spend my 54th, 51st, 28th birthday than doing a play or two.

First show 3 pm. Second 8 pm.

Today, on my 54th, 51st, 28th birthday, the reviews in the papers tell us *Two Keys* is a hit.

> "Tony Walton's auspicious directing debut...he can apparently do anything theatrical supremely well."
> "Bebe Neuwirth will tear your heart apart...mesmerising and compelling."
> "Dee Hoty breathtaking...played with exquisite complexity."

"Bobby Cannavale brilliant in the comparatively small part of the Waiter...a brief dance of delight and desire."

"Leigh Lawson superb, flashes of sheer acting genius... a worthy successor to Coward the actor."

"It was a privilege to be in the audience for this masterful performance."

Am I being immodest in recording this? Yep! Do I care? Nope! Hey. This is America.

And I am 54, 51, 28.

After the show, cast, crew, Twiggs, Ace and Carly, Sybil, Emma et al, appear backstage with a blazing birthday cake. Sing "Happy Birthday" to me. Can't think of any place I'd rather be right now than here.

"... I never knew one moment's peace like this.
Here, in this little soft retreat,
My thoughts unbent from all the cares of life,
Content with fortune..."

Everyone front of house and backstage is wearing a grin. The "House Full" signs are up at every performance. The most successful box office Bay Street Theatre has ever had.

For Tony's directing debut, some awesome figures appear on the scene. Director Mike Nichols flies in for the night. A god. Sidney Lumet, Karel Reisz, Lauren Bacall, Julie Andrews and her husband Blake Edwards, playwrights Lanford Wilson, Terrence McNally, Broadway impresarios and directors, they come backstage and we bask in their praise.

"Jeez," says my new best buddy Bobby, "it's like playing Broadway."

And there is talk of it, a transfer to Broadway. But that's all it can be – talk. Bebe starts rehearsing for a new Broadway production of the musical *Chicago* in a month. Me? I am lost in a midsummer night's day-dream.

My last day at Sag. I dread saying goodbye to my director, cast and crew. We're a family now – stitched together like the old patchwork quilts displayed in the windows of the antique shops as I walk to the theatre to prepare for the final performance.

Past the cosy-looking grey and white clapboard houses with their neat lawns and white picket fences. Along Main Street, drifting by the ornate wooden awning of the American Hotel where we had our wedding breakfast.

Heavy-hearted. Sad to be leaving. I stand in the small court-yard at the entrance to the Bay Street Theatre. The "House Full" signs are up as usual. The poster for our play already looks like yesterday's news – a cartoon of Noël Coward, and above it the title *Noël Coward In Two Keys*. Underneath, in alphabetical order, the names of the cast.

A fat, bald American man, wearing an electric blue Lacoste tennis shirt – stretching over his distended gut and trying desperately to make contact with the fluorescent orange shorts miraculously suspended somewhere beneath the overhang – turns to his wife who is dressed with a similar sense of humour, and says:

"Will ya look at that, honey. *Noël Coward In Two Keys*. Jeez! I thought he was dead."

"Yeah!" muses Fatso's wife. "He must be real old, still got a big followin' though, look, it says sold out."

Standing ovation. Cheers and bravos. And hateful goodbyes.

As I leave the theatre I give Sybil a copy of *Noël and Gertie*. A two-hander compilation of Coward's words and music that I want to adapt and direct with Twiggs starring as Gertie next year at Bay Street. Syb says she'll read it and let me know.

London

FOUR

The flat is strangely quiet and empty. At moments I expect to turn around and see my family – but they're far away in the pink sands and turquoise waters of Bermuda, I hope having fun and missing me desperately.

Solitude. I'm going to need it.

My script for *A Midsummer Night's Dream* prepared, each scene exit and entrance tabbed for easy access. The two parts, Oberon and Theseus, highlighted in individual colours to avoid confusion when learning. Each page is sellotaped into a thick exercise book with room for stage directions either side and fifty blank pages at the back for my notes. This takes a day to prepare.

Over the last three weeks in my daily dementia I've discovered Hugo and Vernon object strongly to the presence of Theseus and Oberon. They just don't get on and make it very difficult for the host: when one couple comes in the room, the others leave.

At present I know about a third of *The Dream*. Familiar with the rest, but won't be, can't be, "books down" by the start of rehearsals in two days' time.

Wracked with a potent mixture of excitement, fear and guilt. Excitement for the unknown, fear for the unknown, guilt for the unknown – lines. Having recently evicted Loveless the lodger, the schizophrenic demanding voices of Hugo and Vernon, and now the megalomaniacal Theseus and Oberon, force me to accept there's only so much my spongy brain will absorb and choose to retain.

The play begins with Theseus, then Oberon takes over, then Theseus returns, then Oberon reappears to close the play. Oberon is the glamorous, sexy part, with some magnificent speeches. The daunting discovery is that word-for-word, demigod Theseus has even more to say for himself than the King of the fucking Fairies, Oberon.

Every waking moment is spent cramming lines until at the end of each day my brain throbs and actually hurts.

I want to learn my Shakespeare with my "ends of lines" as taught by Peter Hall. Basically, at this stage, it involves clicking fingers to help mentally mark the end of a line. If marked by a comma, a breath may be taken. A pause only at a full stop. And most importantly, respecting the iambic pentameter.

I don't enjoy speaking or listening to Shakespeare when the rhythms and the poetry of the lines are ignored. That's the way the poet from Stratford wanted his lines spoken. Your first obligation is to your author – to serve the play – but it is an extra discipline, and I worry: do I have time to cover it all?

It's hard to imagine Sag Harbor even exists now – perhaps it didn't? Perhaps I just dreamt it.

The RSC rehearsal rooms are in an old two-storey building in a not very salubrious part of Clapham North. On the ground floor of the building, director Michael Bogdanov is re-rehearsing and replacing some of the cast for his production of *Faust*, scheduled to play in the Pit Theatre at the same time that we're doing *The Dream* in the main theatre. We're rehearsing on the first floor above them.

When I first enter the building I see Kate Duchene, my leading lady from *The Relapse*. I say thank you God for the friendly, familiar face. She is rehearsing to take over a part in *Faust*. It's common practice at the RSC to re-cast from the company as the season progresses. My old mate of twenty-five years ago, Michael Feast, who is playing Faust, is also there, and I get a warm, giggly welcome from a couple of other familiar faces. I'm feeling happier now. Back in the fold. As I ascend the stairs to our rehearsal room, I suck on a terrified cigarette that transmogrifies to ash in one inhalation. I enter through the double doors marked:

ROYAL SHAKESPEARE COMPANY
A MIDSUMMER NIGHT'S DREAM
REHEARSAL ROOMS
QUIET PLEASE

About twenty people are milling around, talking, laughing, studying their scripts, stretching, warming up, checking props, uninhibited, at home.

This production of *A Midsummer Night's Dream* has been in existence for over a year. It has proved a huge success for the company. Ours is a completely new cast.

Piers Ibbotson, an intense, likeable chap, who has the unenviable task of assistant director, introduces himself and some of the cast to me. Christopher Benjamin from *The Relapse* arrives encased in his motorcycle gear and carrying a crash helmet. Christopher is playing Bottom. We're told by Piers that Adrian Noble won't be here until after lunch and suggest those of us involved read through the opening scene of the play. The others go off to a movement class in the church hall a few hundred yards away in Clapham High Street to rehearse the dances and "fairy scenes".

Puck is played by Ian Hughes. Quite short, about 30 years old, with a tuneful Welsh voice. Amanda Harris is playing Hippolyta and Titania. I like her immediately. In old jeans and T-shirt, petite, blonde, laughing green eyes, confident friendly manner and a smile as wide as Tower Bridge. I'm relieved to find she's still "on the book" and I'm not the only one carrying my script around. She's been with the company on and off for about eight years.

After lunch, Adrian Noble appears. Tall, boyish good looks, he appears to be very relaxed and confident. It's our first meeting and, like me, his first day of rehearsal. Piers has been conducting the previous week's work, concerning himself mainly with the ensemble staged pieces.

The fourteen members of the cast sit in a wide semi-circle around Adrian. His manner is relaxed, positive and assured. A pleasing sense of humour. I sense instinctively he's a director actors can trust. A rarer occurrence than one might imagine.

After the traditional round robin, where each company member introduces themselves and states their role in the production, we're shown the innovative designs for the costumes and set by our brilliantly talented designer, Anthony Ward.

I know already our production has elements of a homage to Peter Brook's landmark production in the early 1970s. The set is minimalistic. Primary colours. Bare stage for the most part, with two ten-foot-high doors that emerge from under the stage for certain scenes. Puck and First Fairy are suspended mid-air on green umbrellas for the opening scene. For the forest scenes, dozens of yellow light bulbs of varying sizes and elevations descend on wires from above the stage. In the second act, when the four lovers fall asleep under Puck's spell, they are wrapped in four large white bodybags and hoisted eight feet into the air and hang suspended there looking like chrysalises before their meta-morphosis into butterflies. For Titania's bower, an enormous padded pink umbrella is lowered to the centre of the stage.

Some costumes have an Eastern influence. Mine, for instance, is a gold brocade Nehru Achkan tunic with gold Maharajah churidar-type trousers, gold slippers, a vast purple silk cloak with hundreds of sequins for Oberon, a heavier and larger gold cloak for Theseus.

The "mechanicals", i.e. Bottom's gang, will be basically garbed in the 1950s period. Adrian suggests this period was the end of an "age of innocence". The mechanicals are also to double as Titania's fairies wearing chiffon blouses and brightly coloured ostrich feather wigs. Titania is in what I can only describe as a Busby Berkeley figure-hugging cabaret gown of pink velvet, hemmed in pink ostrich feathers. The transition from Theseus to Oberon, and Hippolyta to Titania, will be made on stage, by the mere donning of one cloak over another. This immediately worries me. But I'm nonetheless attracted to the concept that the play, the sets, the costumes, transcend time and place. It is a dream after all.

Adrian gives a short introductory speech. He is obviously still intrigued by the play. He says he thinks there is more to discover in this new production, but there are certain things he will want to retain that he considers enriched the previous one. He tells us he thinks it will be a fulfilling, happy experience for us all.

That remains to be seen. My intention is to try and chart the voyage if I can through rehearsals and the London and Stratford run of the play. I suspect the UK and Far East tour will tell a different story altogether. This intention is compounded when we are given an RSC "welcome pack" containing company information and our schedules.

I flick though the schedule, my blood turns cold; first my lips go numb, then the rest of me.

What's this?

Japan – virtually the whole of January into February. Hong Kong – two and a half weeks. Australia and New Zealand – two and a half months.

Oh, my God! – Four and a half *months*, not four and half *weeks*. What a klutz. How could I make such a stupid mistake? Worse – how do I tell my wife I'm such a klutz and I've made such a stupid mistake?

The blame squarely rests with Hugo and Vernon for being so consummately selfish and possessive. How could I be expected to concentrate on such details with those two monumental egos demanding my entire attention day and night?

But, nevertheless, I'm in for an earful when I tell the Missus, I know.

"So, do you want to read through the play?" Adrian asks.

Before anyone else can answer, a voice with a Welsh accent declares –

"Oh, for God's sake, we don't want to read the play again."
So we don't.

I'm disappointed, but too inhibited on my first day to say so.
I assume the voice must be speaking for the rest of the company.
In fact, I discover later in the day that many of the cast would
have liked a read-through, but the moment is gone.

It's not by mistake that rehearsals historically begin with a
read-through. Scary as it always is, it serves a multi-purpose.
It's the first shared experience of performance, evaluations can
be made, a bonding takes place. We all hear the play together
for the first time.

The Welsh voice belongs to Bernard (Bernie) Lloyd, playing
Quince, a greatly respected actor and veteran of some twenty
or more years with the RSC. About sixty years of age I would
guess, a short, compact Welsh physique, and thick white hair.
Bernie whistles a lot. A breathy sort of private whistle as if it's
just for himself. He is by no means the oldest member of the
cast. John Warner, playing Starveling, is 76, I'm told. Not sure
I want to be touring when I'm 76, but who knows? Apparently
his partner of many years died recently and he wants to get
away from his life here for a time. I discover mine isn't the only
faux pas with the schedule; when John discovers that the Gold
Coast he has told his family and friends we are visiting, is not in
fact in Africa, as he thought, but on the east coast of Australia, I
begin to get the distinct impression that whatever the age we're
a band of travelling players – it doesn't actually matter that
much which country we're going to, or for how long. The play's
the thing.

We work some more on the first scene of the play. Some first
scenes of Shakespeare's plays are notoriously difficult. This is
no exception. By the end of the day, we've "blocked" and got it
on its feet. We run the scene several times. It's Theseus' job to
kick it into gear – I can't get him out of neutral.

I write down every move meticulously in my script in stage shorthand. No back of envelope scribbling this time. Precise and clear. If we're going to work at this pace, and it looks as if we are, I'll need to know exactly where I am and what I'm doing when we come back to it.

This familiar, but yet still horrific, irritating, embryonic state. My limbs don't belong to me, my voice is not my own. My mouth is a telephone answering machine. "Hello, we're not here at the moment, please leave your name and number and we'll get back to you as soon as possible, thank you for calling."

My arms and legs feel like sails on a windmill whenever I try to make a gesture or move. I can't walk and talk at the same time with even the remotest feeling of normality.

Always happens at the beginning when trying to host another spirit, inhabit him, or he me, whichever one it turns out to be.

Adrian Noble is a blessing. He has some wonderful moments, focused and fun. He obviously enjoys the rehearsal process. He conjures an atmosphere of trust whereby no one feels inhibited or reluctant to contribute and experiment. Rather, it encourages one to do so. This is the gulf between what makes a good director and a bad director. It's clear he likes actors and doesn't have a fear of them, and a director can't fake that. I've worked with directors that try to pretend they like, trust, and are not afraid, of actors. But there's no fooling a thesp.

On the other hand, I have known actors who would frighten the shit out of Genghis Khan.

On the way home I pass the pub on the corner. Through the window its seductive Rembrandt light and half a dozen of my cast beckon me in, but the custom of a "quickie" after rehearsals now sadly must stop for me. Every minute I can spend with my script has to be cherished. It's my constant companion, sleeps by my bed, and is carried with me everywhere, never farther away from my side than a City broker's mobile phone.

THE DREAM

Just about by the skin of my teeth keeping ahead on my lines. But it's a hard slog. It's the second time in quick succession of learning two huge parts together. I finished *Two Keys* just over a week ago although that all seems like a dream to me now. I hadn't played two characters in one play on stage before *Two Keys*. Now I am doing it again – and it's a bugger.

I ask Adrian what differences I should be looking for when changing from one character to another. Surprisingly, he advises me not to worry too much about that. This throws me. I feel I surely have to find more change in stance, walk, voice, etc, to define an acceptable, if limited, difference. Can the mere changing of a cloak be enough for an audience? For an actor? No, of course it can't. Can it?

When I did a TV series, *Stick with Me, Kid* two years ago for Disney, I played twenty-six different characters with the help of wigs, make-up, costume, etc. In this production, at our point of character change, Oberon and Titania circle upstage, are helped into long golden cloaks over their costumes, and walk downstage as Theseus and Hippolyta. I don't feel anywhere near confident with this change yet. Unless they are very familiar with the play I worry the audience will be confused if there isn't some defining shift in not only costume, but character.

A joy to watch the younger actors at rehearsal. The youngest, playing Demetrius, Matthew Macfadyen, is just 21 years old and left RADA only last year. Tall, handsome, gifted; a born actor. Rebecca Egan tall, willowy and beautiful, with talent to match. She is going to be a perfectly lovely Helena. John Lloyd Fillingham intense, burning with desire as Lysander. Katy Brittain as Hermia looks 20 –

"I'm nearly 30 years old, how long do I have to play virgins?"

– but does it brilliantly anyway. Steven O'Neil as Thisbe is going to be knock-out and very funny, as is Sean McKenzie as Snug. They are all keen and talented and thrilled to be doing what they are doing. And why wouldn't they be?

Ian Hughes is crafting his way through Puck with great skill and commitment, and during Christopher Benjamin's scenes we get glimpses of his Bottom, which seems to be growing daily.

Adrian sits with his script on a wire music stand or on the table at his side, very reminiscent of Peter Hall. He has stopped smoking and tears thin strips of paper from an A4 pad which he then rolls up and chews. I find this little eccentric habit rather touching for some reason. At the end of the day there are dozens of tiny white mouse droppings littered around his chair.

I'm comforted by his constant references to the text. We sit around and meticulously dissect each scene before putting it "on its feet", then gather around his table and dissect again, on occasion counting out the iambic pentameter on our fingers, looking for change, tone, colour, rhythm. Then he'll say –

"Let's practise that again."

The technique he subscribes to for speaking the verse, though not as strictly adhered to as Peter Hall's, is basically the same, thank God. With Adrian one is allowed to bend the rules occasionally by negotiation. In my experience you can negotiate with Peter Hall on virtually everything – but rarely on that.

It's quite staggering how many directors and actors don't seem to know, or refuse to embrace, this concept and discipline. We're told by Adrian,

"People come to the RSC to hear Shakespeare spoken the way it should be spoken, and it's our job to do that."

Even longer rehearsal day tomorrow I'm told. Home to cram the beautiful lines I so want to make mine own.

Speak to Twiggs and the kids every day in Bermuda.

"I've been offered one of the leads in a TV film for CBS," she tells me today.

"Great. How's the script?"

"I liked it. It's fun. A good part for me."

"That's wonderful, darling. Congratulations."

"There's a problem."

"There always is. What is it?"

"Well, two, actually."

Here we go again.

"We start filming in two weeks' time in Wilmington, South Carolina. I'll have to cut Bermuda short, and rearrange flights to get back to London with the kids, and repack."

This proposed holiday seems doomed not to happen one way or another.

"What's the other problem?"

"It's a four-week shoot. We don't wrap till two days after you open in *The Dream*. I wouldn't be there for your First Night."

I say nothing. It's a blow. I want, I need her with me at previews and especially First Night: she's my Geiger counter, my reference – and more importantly, one person at least in the audience who I know will love me no matter how dreadful I might be.

"Hello, are you there?"

"Yeah, I'm here."

"Shall I turn it down?"

"No, of course you must do it. It'll be good for you but I'm disappointed, the timing stinks."

"I know, I'm sorry, but at least I'll be home for ten days before I have to leave."

It's about this point I realise I should seize the opportunity of her obvious feelings of guilt – I haven't yet found the right time, or the right courage, to drop my "mix-up" bombshell concerning the tour dates.

"I've got a bit of bad news too."

"What?"

"I don't know how, but I got the dates wrong for the tour aboard. It's not four-and-a-half-weeks; it's – four-and-a-half-months."

"Don't worry," golden girl says, "we'll work something out. I'm more concerned about the next few weeks."

I congratulate myself on perfect timing. Bomb dropped – no explosion.

The choreography for our play is being done by Sue Lefton. I first met Sue some years ago when I was playing Alec D'Urberville in Roman Polanski's film *Tess*. I know she's tough, Sue that is, not Tess. By tough, I mean she works you hard, very hard. Amanda Harris and I wrapped today at about 8.30 pm after a painful dizzy-making two hours of spinning circles, catching and hoisting Amanda in the air and learning what I suppose to any performer would be considered simple dance routines. My father was a professional dancer, for Christ's sake. Today it became evident to all who witnessed that not a beat of that talent has been genetically passed on to his son.

By the time we finish, exhausted, brain-dead, foot-dead, every corpuscle aches and I'm feeling positively Uncle Dick.

Not a minute of the day is wasted. When not involved in a scene Adrian is rehearsing, or "practising" as he calls it, in the main room, I'm either scheduled for "voice" with our voice coach Lynn Darnley in the basement room, or blocking new scenes in the church hall up the road, running backwards and forwards and up and down the street and up and down the stairs like the proverbial blue-arsed fly.

I've had to restructure my day to accommodate some more time for line study. By the time I've travelled home from rehearsal, quickly showered, phoned the Bermuda Triangle, recapped on the day's work, my brain is as scrambled as the eggs I've cooked for supper. If I then sit for an hour until after midnight to learn my lines, my complaining cranium becomes a sort of engorged sponge and refuses to accept them as friends.

So my routine now is to try and get six or seven hours' sleep, wake about 6 am, and work for three hours before leaving for rehearsal. I can learn much more this way. Of course, my memory circuit still plays that amusing little game of letting me believe I'm word perfect until rehearsal, when any onlooker might be forgiven for thinking I hadn't looked at the text for a week.

Last day of first week of rehearsal. Adrian has restructured the play from five acts into two with one interval. We have roughly blocked and touched on every scene in the play except the huge scene in our Act Two when the courtiers watch the play-within-the-play performed by the "mechanicals". To have achieved this in a week, well six days, is, we all agree, a monumental achievement. But we haven't even started the assault on the summit. We're still in the foothills.

Despite what his Mastership, the great Noël Coward, felt about rehearsals – he is reputed to have said "Just learn your lines and don't bump into the furniture, dear", always insisting that his cast were word perfect before the rehearsals commenced – I'm finding the practice an unsatisfying ordeal, and not in the least conducive to the creative rehearsal process. It feels horribly rushed. And it frightens me that I don't have enough time to go back for private exploration, only remembering moves, bashing lines into my addled skull.

It's a relief under these circumstances and time limitations not to have to "find" the blocking, and to my surprise and relief most of the suggested staging works amazingly well for me and feels right and comfortable. It's a framework I can adjust to serve me.

We have two and a half weeks to go before the first preview. To have roughly worked through most of the play like this by the end of the first week would have been impossible without this routine and scaffolding, but even so I feel like I've just run the London Marathon.

I can truly say everyone is absolutely exhausted. There is a growing feeling among some of the cast, particularly some of the younger ones, that we are being squeezed into a mould of what the production was before – a feeling that they are being denied the right to explore. I understand what they are feeling but today found an opportunity to, I hope, reassure them and clear away some doubts. I'm convinced it's only with this process in place that we have a hope in hell of getting an extraordinarily complicated and very technical production like this ready to see in the time left to us. And anyway, I don't want any dissension in the cast. The only way this can work is with the whole company pulling this fucker up the hill together as a team.

A hard core of us are even now amazed at just how very well we all get on and work together. GCMs – Good Company Members? Or FIAs – Friends In Adversity?

"Do you think we'll all be getting on this well in ten months' time?" someone asked today during the coffee break. I feel part of my job is to make sure, as far as possible, that we do.

I spend Sunday alone. A golden empty space to fill with the increasingly daunting task of learning and making friends with some of Oberon and Theseus' long speeches in the second half of the play. Didn't leave the flat. Spent seventeen hours working on the play and seven hours dreaming it.

This isn't my first encounter with Theseus. I played the part three years ago in an audio recording for Peter Hall using Mendelssohn's music. He assembled a cast from his days at the National Theatre and the RSC, and we did an edited version of the play in a sound studio. Two years later, Ian Judge, who directed *The Relapse* last season at the RSC, was searching for a piece of music from his collection and by mistake pulled out our recording, saw my name on the cover, remembered seeing me in Peter Hall's production of Peter Shaffer's play *Yonadab* at the National Theatre nine years earlier, and cast me in *The Relapse* where this story began. Work finds work.

Rather ungratefully, perhaps, I've always thought of Theseus as a bit of a boring old fart. Shakespeare, with his fearless chutzpah and ingenuity of a master storyteller supreme, transposes Theseus, the minotaur slayer in Greek mythology, to almost that of an English country squire. But he shouldn't, mustn't, can't, be a boring old fart. In trying to win the love of his captive Hippolyta he has a similar journey to Oberon who is seeking to re-ignite Titania's devotion. If one brings Theseus' mythological Greek deeds from his previous, heroic life, onto the stage in the new courts and green glades of England, he too should have a new vibrant presence. This has to be found. I'm discovering it's all in there, in the text: his authority, control, sensitivity, and sexiness, yes, and humour.

I'm still finding it a bugger to learn. At the end of each rehearsal day, our kindly and immensely supportive DSM, Kate Vinnicombe, gives us a list of our mistakes in the text, every word, full stop, and comma. Her arduous task is a tremendous help and much appreciated. At the moment I plough on in the rough, knowing I have to come back and pick out the weeds and stones later. The actual process of learning lines is one of the less exhilarating aspects of an actor's life, a self-disciplined slog, culminating in a delirious euphoria of disbelief that one has conquered the beast and can move on to the fun part of the job. I haven't got to the fun part yet.

Will I ever get to the fun part?

The week merges into one long day with breaks for sleeping.

It's beginning to happen, I see me going there, that familiar weird and wonderful no man's land. The twilight zone. Nothing's real any more, or nothing that is real, seems real, or attaches any importance. Things that aren't real are my reality now; newspapers never so much as glanced at; television screens remain as grey as the future.

Bizarre dreams haunt my sleep.

Last night I was the carcass of a new car on an assembly line in a factory in Coventry, newly sprayed but without wheels or engine. Men in overalls pulled down spider-leg machinery to bolt on my doors, fix my headlights, arrange my chrome trim. Workers in overalls and black glass masks, sparks flying, weld my seats into place and behind me the other cars on the assembly line are Demetrius, Lysander, Hippolyta, Puck and Bottom. All this dreamed as a black and white 1950s Movietone newsreel, with the commentator's strident voice trying to convince the nation that "Britain is on the move again".

Several nights of the classic actor's dream: finding myself naked on the wrong stage in the wrong play, not knowing a word of my part. All as vivid and real and terrifying as the very vivid and real and terrifying possibility that in two short weeks I stand naked on the wrong stage, in the wrong play, not knowing a word of my part.

Lynn Darnley, our voice coach, is a godsend. Rehearsals are scheduled so that each leading member of the cast gets at least an hour a day to work with her. Her infinite patience astonishes me. Her knowledge of the text and sympathy to the actors' problems moves her role way beyond that of a voice coach.

In her one-on-one classes, apart from a vocal warm-up, we do exercises called "little games" such as throwing a ball to each other to mark the ends of lines whilst doing a speech from the play. Or putting two chairs side by side and as I recite a speech I move from one to the other sitting at each punctuation mark. Sounds simple – the mental concentration makes my brain ache and, after half and hour moving to and fro, my legs feel like plastic tubes filled with hot water. Other games consist of moving chairs around a room at a point of emphasis in the text. More ball-throwing to place the points to take a breath, or run on through a phrase. Strange as they may sound, in practice these exercises are immensely useful in correlating a physical memory to the textual memory.

You don't fall into this sort of care and tuition somewhere other than the RSC. Not in my experience, anyway. We get more support than a boxer's bollocks. But the old barbarians are knocking at the gates and the actor's war cry goes up:

"If only we had more time."

I am at the stage now as an actor in rehearsals where I need to metaphorically go away for a time, to return later when it's all over. It's the only way. There is no choice. The play's the thing. This, sadly, won't be a problem for us as Twiggs leaves for Carolina in two days to start filming.

I have two major bêtes noires at present. One is the switch from iambic pentameter to the older Anglo Saxon, four-beats-a-line Shakespeare uses for Oberon's penultimate and final speeches. I'm finding the change maddeningly difficult for some reason. The other, even more confusing, is Theseus' famous "Imagination" speech in our Act Two. My actor's instinct, in the form of a small flashing red light and whispered voice in the back of my word-weary brain, insists something is wrong with the speech. It seems to have been tampered with, it doesn't flow, it's confused and confusing, the lineation is disturbed, and if I can't understand it, my brain refuses to accept it and let it in. However hard I try to bash the door down a still small voice whispers:

"No, you can't come in here until I completely trust and understand you."

Here's the problem. Theseus says –

> "More strange than true. I never may believe
> These antique fables, nor these fairy toys.
> Lovers and madmen have such seething brains,
> Such shaping fantasies, that apprehend
> More than cool reason ever comprehends.
> The lunatic, the lover, and the poet
> Are of imagination all compact.
> One sees more devils than a vast hell can hold,
> That is, the madman: the lover, all as frantic,
> Sees Helen's beauty in a brow of Egypt:
> The poet's eye, in a fine frenzy rolling,
> Doth glance from heaven to earth, from earth to
>   Heaven;

And as imagination bodies forth
The forms of things unknown, the poet's pen
Turns them to shapes, and gives to airy nothing
A local habitation and a name.
Such tricks hath strong imagination,
That if it would but apprehend some joy
It comprehends some bringer of that joy;
Or in the night, imagining some fear,
How easy is a bush supposed a bear."

Nothing wrong with that, no cause for flashing lights and whispered still small voices. Or is there? So what's the problem? The problem is – in line six, the author decides to introduce himself – the poet,

"The lunatic, the lover, and the poet"

and then at line eleven inserts,

"The poet's eye, in a frenzy rolling..." etc.

Brilliant stuff. Exhilarating imagery but the feel is different. His style has changed. It jars and lacks his usual elegance in dovetailing such thoughts together. There's an incongruity about it and my instinct screams out that it must have been tampered with or put in later, maybe as a last minute sort of in-joke with his audience. Tradition has it that Shakespeare played Quince but perhaps Shakespeare played Theseus at some time and inserted these lines? But for one already confused mouthpiece, it presents an incongruity I could do without at this point.

We rehearse Act Two.
"When listening I come in and out of the Imagination speech, Leigh," Adrian says during a one-on-one note session, towards the end of the day.
"You start all right, then I lose you, then I find you again."

"That's because there's something strange about parts of this speech, it just isn't right," I impugn.

"The style is different. Shakespeare seems to be saying two different things expecting us to accept they're the same."

"Let's try a little game," Adrian suggests.

"Do the speech and I'll interrupt you and ask questions, to see if it clarifies anything – just for fun."

I sit at the corner of Adrian's table. He tears a strip from his A4 pad to chew on.

> Me: "More strange than true."
> A: "More what?"
> Me: "Strange than true. I never may believe these antique fables."
> A: "You don't believe what?"
> Me: "I never may believe these antique fables and these fairy toys."
> A: "Why?"
> Me: "Lovers and madmen have such seething brains."
> A: "Who have?"
> Me: "Lovers and madmen..."

And while Adrian creates a little snow flurry of masticated A4 pellets around him, I gnaw away at the text.

I look forward each day to rehearsing with him. He not only makes rehearsals fun, but his polymathic mind is tremendously inventive and he possesses the rare gift of conveying clearly and succinctly his concepts to his actors.

It's very hot and this morning I arrived at rehearsal to find him stripped to the waist, working through a scene with the Mechanicals, up and down the rehearsal room, back and forth like a hod carrier on a building site.

My two ex-best mates, Vernon and Hugo, who unfortunately insisted on travelling from Sag Harbor back to London with me, have with much persuasion and hint-dropping packed their bags and moved out. I now spend my waking hours, my meals, my toilet, my shower, my tube ride, my taxi, my bed, with my two new best friends, Theseus and Oberon.

Vernon and Hugo and I used to visit a small theatre book-shop a few happy steps from the theatre in Sag Harbor. There Vernon and Hugo would persuade me to buy all the Noël Coward books I could find, some old, some new.

Theseus and Oberon would visit occasionally and we would buy copies of *A Midsummer Night's Dream* and any relevant Shakespeare text books, old or new, that we saw on the shelves.

When I arrived back in England I had a large suitcase full of books. The trouble with fantasy friends is that they don't help you carry the luggage.

I was sitting on the tube with Oberon and Theseus on our way home tonight looking through one of the books we found in the second-hand bookshop in Sag Harbor, a not very thrilling academic textbook, when Theseus, sitting on my left, peers over my shoulder and, referring to my book, says,

"Look at that, that's interesting."

"What? What?" I say with growing irritation at the constant interruption in every little thing I try to do or read.

"That – look at that."

"Fuck me," says Oberon aloud from my right but using my mouth to say it. The only other person in the carriage is an attractive young black lady sitting opposite us; she looks up and with a single blink makes it clear she isn't interested in the proposition.

"Sorry," I mumble, "Something I was reading."

She smiles.

But Oberon's right – "Fuck me – There it is."

The writer of the book says of a Shakespearean scholar, a geezer called Dover Wilson, "his brilliant detection of revisions, especially his identifying of an *addition*, the lines about the imagination of the poet...his conviction that the lines on the poet are of a *much later date* than those on the lunatic and the lover mainly from his impression of their style."

Vindication! Oh what a clever boy am I.

"Always trust your instincts," I tell Obe' and Thes' as we exit the station.

But of course if I'd had more time for research instead of having to cram it in between cramming in line learning, I'd have realised all this earlier.

It doesn't change the speech, I've still got to do it as written. But it changes my approach to it radically. It clears the path. I no longer have to flaff around feeling inept and inadequate. This confirmation of my instinctive suspicions gives me the confidence and courage to embrace the problem and find my way back onto the highway despite being given confused directions by the author of the lines, whoever wrote them and whenever they were written.

When we arrive home, Twiggs is packing for Carolina. I tell her the emotional news. She doesn't appear to be as moved as us. It's only a small blip in a big speech after all, I suppose. But to Oberon, Theseus and me it's one less problem out of the way and gives a quite unreasonable but much needed boost to the confidence in my "still, small voice".

Heartbreaking to see my wife packing her suitcase again.

During one-on-one rehearsals today Adrian says:

"What if Oberon is Theseus' alter ego?"

A very exciting idea. It means I can do anything I want. Anything. It's totally freeing. It means changing on stage from one character to another is legit. It means anything I do can be Theseus' imagination or fantasy. That leads me to think what if the whole play is Theseus' dream?

What if the whole thing is Hippolyta's dream? Or Bottom's dream?

Hang on. – If it's a dream I have no restrictions, we have no restrictions, anything can happen in a dream. Once you accept you're in a dream there are no limitations, there are no rules, no boundaries.

> "And as imagination bodies forth
>   The forms of things unknown, the poet's pen
>   Turns them to shapes, and gives to airy nothing
>   A local habitation and a name.
>   Such tricks hath strong imagination."

FIVE

This is an horrendously technical show, two days of tech-ing long into the night, hour upon hour trying to get doors to rise and fall, lights to rise and fall, body-bags to rise and fall, spirits not to.

After several costume fittings and wig fittings, a clear image of how I should look begins to emerge. At least on this vital issue I am clear. An element of a wild animal: a lion seems to suit for Oberon, a stag perhaps for Theseus. And if they're a colour Oberon is purple or blue, Theseus gold. This is preordained by my costumes and happily suits me fine. I've been using Oberon's vast purple sequinned cloak all through rehearsal so this presents no tripping-over problems in performance on stage. At dress rehearsal my leonine-influenced appearance for Oberon receives the encouraging approval of director and cast, feels good, feels right, looks right, wild hair, darkened beard, visually strong and commanding for both parts. But not, alas, for our designer.

There are five or six designers that are as important, and contribute as much, to the success of the production as a director or cast. Anthony Ward, our designer, is one of the five or six. I admire this man. He has a brilliance in his work and I like him but he's of the opinion my look is too wild. He wants Oberon's and Theseus' appearance "more sophisticated".

"I don't want sophisticated," I emphasise in my dressing room at the end of the gruelling day.

"Would you consider shaving your beard off?" he ventures.

The very thought fills me with horror and all sorts of insecurities. Since Day One I've never for a moment questioned that Oberon and Theseus wear a beard. They are the only characters in the play who do and for me it helps somehow display an authority essential to both parts. A minor point? Trivial? Not at all: the external vision sparks the internal fire.

Eventually, as usual, a compromise is reached. Less wild, but with a beard and some make-up to emphasise the eyes. We also reach an agreement that about a yard be taken out of my very baggy gold, maharajah-type trousers from around the posterior and crotch, which I felt a necessary measure for reassuring the first preview audience that, however real the possibility, I have not in fact crapped my pants.

I have no idea what the date is or even the month – no idea. It could be August, it could be September. Doesn't matter. What I sure as hell do know is that we open tomorrow night. Actual dates ceased to have any significance some time ago. All that has mattered is the rehearsal call sheet, my schedule telling me when I'm called and what the scenes are. I don't read dates, Greenwich Mean Time is not my Mean Time.

If I were to be absolutely and totally honest with myself about how I feel, I'd have to say "I'm scared shitless at the thought". But I have no intention of being absolutely and totally honest with myself. In fact I have every intention of lying through the teeth to myself. I feel I must at least appear confident, I see no other way for there to be the remotest possibility of me stepping out on the Barbican stage tomorrow night. We've had a week of previews. Previews are immensely informative and reward-ing to any director worth his salt and any cast worth theirs. For the first time, you have an audience telling you what *they* think, quite different from the cocooned security of the rehearsal room.

On stage your antennae swish around picking up every station in the cosmos, every signal on the airwaves. Listening to the audience. Listening to your mates on stage. Seeing them try their very best. Playing your part:

"Dare I try this like this? Oh, fuck it, have a go."

"Oh Christ! That didn't work, never mind, get it tomorrow, onto the next bit."

"Is this working? Is this working? Oh, fuck, thank you God, they're laughing, oh, my Christ, they're clapping."

Tuning into the lights, the new costumes, the new sound, some of which we saw or wore or heard on the last day of Previews for the first time. Plotting the costume changes, the exits and entrances that never appear to remotely resemble the geography of the strips of orange sticky tape mapping them out on the rehearsal room floor.

"What's this, an actual door to open?"

"Will I find the right spot to stand on and be magically elevated ten feet in the air?"

"What's this, a real swing to swing on?"

"What's this, a real goblet? Not a plastic cup."

Surfing the net with two thousand people looking on. www. helpme.barbican.com. Adrenaline rush. The director sitting in the auditorium or the actor on stage, listening, watching, anticipation, longing to learn what they can tell us.

"That's good."

"That isn't."

"That works."

"That don't."

Full houses, several rounds, and standing ovations at the curtain calls.

Backstage after the first Preview, Adrian is extremely pleased and says –

"A good first meeting with the audience. Let's keep practising."

His approval and enthusiasm are the life-pulse at this point. It's as if it were the first time he'd discovered the play. At the daily rehearsal call he speaks of the potency of Shakespeare. Of being aware and not afraid of being intoxicated by it and offering the cup to the audience. Of the enchantment and magic of the play, of renewed awareness, of conflicting atmospheres to bring on stage. He speaks of the plumbing of the piece:

"Turn a tap on here, the water comes out over there; turn it high; turn it low; add hot to cold; cold to hot; mix the temperatures."

Whatever Movietone dream an actor may have lived through nothing can prepare, nothing can second-guess out of the trillion possibilities and therefore probabilities, what is going to go wrong on stage. But you can bet your arse something will.

After my discussion with Anthony Ward, the yards of unwanted fabric hanging around my bum and crotch are eventually removed but baggy gold trousers seem to have proffered a problem all round at the first Preview. Most notably those worn by Ian Hughes as Puck.

There's a point in our production where as a penance for misbehaving, Puck drops his baggy, gold trousers to his ankles revealing underneath a pair of black ostrich feather bloomers that appear to be part of his body. He then bends over for Oberon to pluck from Puck's posterior a fistful of feathers as punishment. Puck screams with pain which turns into a sort of camp Kenneth Williams mince of mischievous pleasure accompanied by an even camper Frankie Howerd whine of sexual relish. Ian does it superbly. The audience love this almost music-hall bit of biz. The laughter went on for so long it was unnerving, and ended in a spontaneous round of applause. When this very satisfying moment on both sides of the footlights is over, Puck pulls up his gold baggies and zips up his fly.

There is then supposed to be a complete change of mood as Oberon gives a long instructional monologue.

Oberon follows this with a quite short but enchantingly magical speech, beloved by me and Oberon, beginning:

> "But we are spirits of another sort.
> I with the morning's love have oft made sport
> And like a forester the groves may tread
> Even 'til the eastern gate, all fiery red,
> Opening on Neptune with fair blessed beams,
> Turns into yellow gold his salt green streams."

I've been looking forward to this little gem. At the moment one of my all too infrequent base camps along the climb. The gift of an ageless, exquisitely composed poem to recite in the middle of the play, magical imagery for all to thrill to.

Now, I've rather under-described the newly-made, first-Preview, as-yet-untried, black ostrich feather bloomers that Puck wears under his gold baggies. Once the waistband is undone, the zip fly released, and the gold baggies are down round his ankles, the feather bloomers make their theatrical debut. The terrified huge bush of feathers seem to spring into a life entirely of their own, like a massive great black sea anemone that has somehow affixed itself around Puck's loins – I swear they're alive.

Nevertheless, all works well until the "music hall gag" is over, and I cross downstage to begin the first of my two beautiful, life-changing speeches. Puck, standing upstage, hoists up the gold baggies and fastens the waistband. But the alarmingly animated feathers refuse to disappear into his gaping fly. At this point, I'm strutting my stuff downstage as best I can, confused by the continuing audience laughter during my not remotely amusing first speech. A few lines into the speech I glance upstage and see Ian frantically struggling with the star-struck feathers. But the more he tries to ram them into his baggy fly, the more deter-mined they appear to be to stay out, and cling to his retreating fingers like a horde of bloodthirsty leeches. In they go, out they come. In they go again, out they spray again. If he turns upstage with his back to the audience, his activities look even more suspect. There's no doubt this is riveting theatre. There is also no doubt I don't have a fart in a storm's chance of ever being heard over the audience's increasingly hysterical laughter.

Eventually Ian is forced to accept the task is futile. "We are staying out", nod the feathers to me as a defeated Ian walks downstage to join Oberon with his protruding bush now an electrically charged, demented black posy of feathery pubic hair swaying back and forth from his unzippable fly. But I've got a very long, serious speech to do. Not only do I have a very long, serious speech to do, but I'm supposed to do it downstage centre, facing out front, with Puck standing beside me, my arm around his shoulder. You couldn't have a more prominent position on stage to stand and display a forest of shuddering, overexcited, black, feathery pubes sticking out of your fly. By now, the audience are apoplectic with mirth, cannons of near-hysterical laughter ricochet around the auditorium.

There's a voice speaking. It could be mine. It's saying my lines. Mouth is on automatic, unheard iambic pentameters tumbling out like sewage being dumped into the ocean. I could be saying "Ladies and Gentlemen, there is a fire, would you please vacate the building" and no one would hear.

A thought, in the form of a neon sign flashes: "envelop him in your cloak, it's your only chance to obscure the offending protrusion". I do. It brings the house down. A frightening roar of delight. An unwanted round of applause. I can now see people on the front row rocking with laughter. If I were in the audience, I'd do the same, and by now I wish I was. But still a small vain, ridiculously optimistic fantasy that the quivering pubic bush will magically disappear before I reach my enchantingly magical poem.

It doesn't.

Everywhere I look "Gremlins Rule OK" is graffitied around the auditorium and stage, and "enchantingly magical" has to be traded for "hopelessly bollocksed", and now all I want to do is arrive at the point in the script that says "Exit Oberon". When I do, I find every member of the cast and crew convulsed with mirth in the wings as we watch Ian on stage alone struggling with the quivering pubic bush and to get to the end of the scene. He does. The audience clapometer reaches a new high.

One of the jigsaw of unnerving possibilities, as you stand in the wings waiting to make an entrance, is the inevitability of this sort of solecism. There is rarely a precedent to draw on to control or resolve such conspiracies. The infamous theatre gremlins are infinitely resourceful and inventive in their quest for fun, or sometimes tragedy, rarely reproducing the same humiliation twice.

A rather gruelling week, rehearsing during the day, performing in previews, matinees and evenings. We have full houses of delightful audiences and the peculiarly comforting feel of family suffuses the auditorium. A warmth spills from them like a floodlight onto the stage. They appear to be familiar with the cast, the text, and even on occasion the production itself, I've never felt this familiarity previously; it's as if the audience almost consider themselves to be part of the company.

Each day we work to incorporate and refine what we receive from them, and from our director's meticulous notes. A small move, a speech inflexion, a sound cue, a light cue, adjusting, refining, until it is orchestrated to as near-perfect as the gremlins will allow. The individual characteristics of my identical friends Oberon and Theseus that began to tentatively emerge in rehearsal now have a self-confidence in their individual identity. Oberon has taken to wearing gold loop earrings that Theseus wouldn't be seen dead in. Twin Theseus has quite a different approach to life than twin Oberon. A different speech pattern, tone, stance and walk, and an altogether different view of life begins to emerge. We still have much more to discover about each other, but we're getting there.

The multi-layered complexity of the story is clarifying at each performance, like an image in a fortune-teller's crystal ball.

This is it. This is why I became an actor, to work in theatre on good plays with people dedicated to their craft. I desperately don't want to let them down. I want to justify the faith in me shown by Maggie and John in the casting department, and my director in casting me. And I don't want to let my cast down. They are "The Dream Team" in more ways than the obvious. Any director would chew his way through an entire A4 notepad to have a company like this. The commitment is total. As bonded as freedom fighters. Backstage we discuss changes and assault plans to surprise the friendly foe. Strategies are adjusted and revised continually in the wings. Old campaigners sought out for advice and young recruits encouraged to be brave. We are learning from and supporting each other. I feel exceedingly proud and privileged to be ranked amongst them.

On the whole, there is very little dissension in the company. I feel instinctively there is maybe a small cell of ego-fed complainers. There always are one or two in any company who need conflict to sustain their paranoia or self-doubt. But the unselfish commitment of the majority submits them to silence. If I've picked up the faintest scent of rabies infiltrating our warren, I'm at it like a ferret down a rabbit's burrow. Discontent can spread like a virus through a company and one can usually trace it to a single source of infection. Immunisation is essential.

We are all a little surprised at just how very funny and accessible this production is to our packed and appreciative audiences. We suspect strongly we are in something good. A rock to build on. But still, for me, a maddening fluctuating barometer of hot to cold, wet to dry, in trying to make some of the more famous arias truly mine own. I hear hollow echoes of great voices past that interrupt and intimidate me during, I suppose, the most famous of Oberon's arias.

"I know a bank where the wild thyme blows..."

I hear Irving, Garrick, Kean, Wolfit and Gielgud bellow in unison from up in the flies: "No, not like that you pretentious prat." The ever-present echo of the vehement alcohol-fuelled voice of a father, now long dead, hell-bent on discouraging any glimmer of self-confidence in his cripplingly shy son, still has a resonance many successes later. But I recognise a steely strength in the small boy that says,

"Enough already. I'll show you fuckers."

Well, will I?

SIX

"Whence are we, and why are we?
Of what scene
The actors or spectators?"

Shelley

Now I cannot describe to you the amount of energy flying around backstage on a first night before an audience. It could fuel a rocket ship to another universe, and sometimes does.

We're appearing on the stage of the main auditorium at the Barbican Theatre so the lead actors get their own dressing room. I'm grateful for the relative solitude. Relative. Because there are more knocks at my dressing room door than a sea port brothel when the fleet's in. People in and out with wigs, make-up, bits of costume. Well-wishers from the company bob heads around the door –

"Good luck, break a leg."

"Sock it to 'em."

"Give 'em hell."

"Be wonderful."

"Yeah, thanks, you too." Phoney bravado fooling no one.

An expectant, altogether over-optimistic row of champagne bottles stand in line on my dressing room table. They stare back at me though the mirror, watching me, like Row A in the stalls. My tamed leonine wig is glued and pinned into place and my trembling fingers attempt to target a black liner pencil under my eye rather than in it. Bouquets of flowers populate the room like a funeral parlour at the demise of someone once much cared for. The fragrance of a huge basket of pink roses and yellow freesias from my much loved, much missed golden girl across the sea, let me know she is with me in spirit – but I'd prefer a hug.

First Night cards and telegrams waiting to be blue-tacked around the walls, marking my kingdom for as long as it's mine like a tom cat sprays his territory.

A cacophony of sound from the corridor and other dressing rooms. Nervous overloud laughter, quickly articulated speech exercises, musical scales, high Cs, and jungle noises waft beneath my door to mingle with the intoxicating cocktail of telegrams, make-up, flowers and fear.

Zipped, buttoned and press-studded into my virgin stiff gold Theseus costume and shoes, I stand before the full length mirror in my brothel, gazing at the unfamiliar reflection, and catch a glimpse of Oberon's huge purple cloak hanging in the corner, its thousand sequinned eyes winking tauntingly at me.

I light a fag. Is this how it feels to pull on your last cigarette before they march you down Death Row?

Comes a voice over the speaker:

"Firing squad ready, prisoner stand against the wall."

Or was it:

"Stand by please, this is your five minute call."

Last rites – a throat lozenge, a sip of Lucozade.

"Beginners please. Miss Harris, Mr Lawson, Mr Hughes, this is your beginners call."

"Good luck", call voices from the other cells as I glide comatose along Death Row to the place of execution.

I've been told that the trauma for an actor on a First Night is equivalent to that of being involved in a major car crash. I don't know who worked that one out. I liken the occasion more to one of being shot on your birthday.

Festooned backstage by greetings, telegrams, cards, bottles of champagne, bouquets of flowers, a walk down Death Row, then, blindfolded by fear, face the firing squad.

Why do we do it?

A few years ago I was fortunate enough to play Antonio in Peter Hall's production of *The Merchant of Venice*, first in London then on Broadway. During that time I became friends with Dustin Hoffman who was playing Shylock. He's passionate about his craft, he'd just won an Oscar for *Rain Man*, it was incredibly brave of him to come over to London and join a British company to play Shylock. Working with him was like working with Santa Claus except it was Christmas every day. One day, he and I were discussing "Why do we do it?". He told me that when he was filming *Marathon Man* with Laurence Olivier, he asked Olivier,

"Why do we do it?"

Olivier's reply was:

"Look at me, look at me, look at me, look at me."

A bit simplistic? Or was Olivier taking the piss? I worked with him once and noticed a slight cruelty at times in his humour. But that's another story. I've no doubt there's a performing gene in many of us "look ats". But it isn't nearly enough of an explanation for the whole attraction, mystery, love of drama, and bizarre choice of profession.

An old mate of mine, Bruce Robinson, decided to stop being an actor when he was 30 to become a writer. When asked why, he told me because he loved words and thought being an actor was his access to them until he realised he didn't want to say somebody else's, he wanted to write his own. Bruce was a successful, talented actor and at the time I thought his change in direction an incredibly brave, possibly foolhardy, decision. Since then his love of language and story-telling has given us *The Killing Fields, Withnail and I, How to Get Ahead in Advertising*, and his novel *The Peculiar Memories of Thomas Penman*. To my certain knowledge he hasn't missed being a "look at" in over twenty years.

For me the mystery began at about age six; my initial attraction to acting in a school play was escape, escape into someone else, into someone else's thoughts and persona, someone else's world and words. A much simpler process when as a child playing fantasy games and having fantasy friends is normal. Vital for an actor to keep the child in him or her alive. Not at all unusual in an artist of any kind. A composer of music, painter, dancer, singer, actor, writer, much more than seeking to be looked at seek a door through which to escape into another world. The audience or listener escapes vicariously through the artist. It's the difference between us and them. It marks you out early, to be cursed or blessed with imagination enough to "channel". Literature, poetry, can inspire a painter to paint a picture, a composer to write a song or symphony. O'Shaughnessy says:

"We are the dreamers of dreams
Wandering by lone sea-breakers,
And sitting by desolate streams –
World-losers and world-forsakers,
On whom the pale moon gleams."

The plays I listen to regularly on the radio, often written and performed by our very best, are not saying "look at me", they're saying "listen to me".

Someone once said they preferred plays on the radio because the pictures are better. Words paint pictures grown out of our most primitive communications. We come into the world through rhythms, we live through rhythms; words into rhythms, into chants, into music, into poetry, into religious ritual, into drama. There is a religiosity still in drama, hard to define this long time past; nevertheless, it's in the DNA of theatre.

Why do we do it?

"In the end, you don't choose it – it chooses you," Dustin says with a smile.

These thoughts remind me of the night the greatest actor of his age, Laurence Olivier, died. It had been of some concern to Dustin during the run of the play that a London West End audience could very rarely be persuaded to its feet during the applause at the end of the show, unlike New York where a standing ovation is quite common if you're in a hit show. On the day Olivier died, a directive went out to all West End Theatres to observe a two-minute silence at the end of the performance in honour of the great man. After the applause the announcement was made and what seemed like an incredibly long two-minute silence ensued – when it was over, the entire house rose to its feet and applauded the memory of the greatest actor of his time. As we left the stage, Dustin with cheeky grin turned to me and whispered,

"Is that what you have to do in this country to get a standing ovation, fucking die?"

When we transferred to Broadway we got a standing ovation every night, even if no one had died.

Back on Death Row, I stand in the wings, and wish I had them. Our stage manager approaches my cowed figure trying to be invisible in a dark corner.

"Why are you hiding behind the bike shed trying to bunk Maths, Lawson?" she says.

Or was it:

"Take your position, please, and stand by for the red light to flash on"?

Please God, if there is one, don't make me go out on that stage tonight. I'll try to believe in you whether you exist or not. I'll stop swearing. I'll never lie again. I'll ring my mother more often. Please let there be a fire, a bomb scare, a death, even mine. I hear the first notes of Ilona Sekacz's hauntingly uplifting music. It's a death march. Sudden hush of the bloodthirsty crowd waiting for the condemned to appear.

There is a God.

Inspiration. Pretend to faint. Do it. Do it now. A red light flashes, I open a door and I'm on stage.

"Now, fair Hippolyta, our nuptial hour"
No comma no full stop so no breath slight upward inflection carry the energy through

"Draws on a pace,"
Snatch top-up breath carry through

"Four happy days bring in"
Same breath vocal energy carry through

"Another moon – but O, methinks, how slow"
Carry through the same breath

"This old moon wanes."
Throw ball, change chairs

Am I on fast-forward or seek-find or both? I swirl upstage to face Amanda sitting on the swing, a reassuring 20,000-watt smile lights up her area of the stage:

"Four days will quickly step themselves in night;
Four nights will quickly dream away the time;
And then the moon, like to a silver bow
New bent in Heaven, shall behold the night
Of our solemnities."

I have no recollection of what followed, none at all. I can't even remember the interval. I'm told we had bravos, cheers, whistles and took six triumphant curtain calls.

I'd like to have remembered that bit.

My replay button only starts the tape as a smiling Adrian enters my dressing room after the show, and we have a few minutes alone to crack a bottle of bubbly, get a few notes, get a bit pissed, get a bit sentimental, get a chance to say thank you.

At the sea port brothel, First Nighters steaming in and out of my dressing room or squeezing for a place to moor between dressers tugging at costumes, and rescuing sweat-soaked wigs like drowning kittens, bums balancing precariously on arms of chairs, sipping champagne. Ace, my altogether amazing son, hugs his Pah enough to make up for the two missing members of our family. I thank God for his presence and for a small group of loving friends whose kindness in being here to offer support this evening quite overwhelms me.

A few bottles of bubbles later, we all trundle up to the foyer bar where the enchanting Maggie Lunn and her casting department reaffirm their excellent good taste in casting us by throwing a party for the company. My friend and agent Michael Foster tells me he's seen *The Dream* twice a year for the past thirteen years and my Oberon is the best he's ever seen. My mate Rupert Penry-Jones makes some useful observations and encourages me to pursue *my* dream. Others say they prefer our production to the original: funnier, more chemistry.

Why not believe them? Just for tonight anyway.

Privately, despite the praise, the flattery, I don't feel I scaled the heights as I should have, could have. I'm not there yet, I'm getting there and I will. I know what I have to do.

All the same, I had to pull a few tricks out of my twenty-five year-old acting bag to get through tonight, and I don't like having to rely on that. My private feeling is I made some breakthroughs, I got my feet off the ground a few times, jumped high, but didn't fly. The frustration is in knowing where I could go with two more weeks rehearsal, or even one, in a rehearsal room, a safe arena to make a prat of myself. It's a much, much slower process to get there once you've opened: the risk of making changes or trying something fundamentally new in public has to be tempered by gentler degrees for the audience and your fellow actors' sake. But I have no choice.

Oberon and Theseus are not as easily accessible as Vernon and Hugo. Snobbish in a way. They don't give trust or make friends as easily. They give and withdraw random reinforcement – aggressive passive. Vernon and Hugo were so separate, Theseus and Oberon mesh into a complicated oneness.

After the party in the foyer bar, to a restaurant with Son and friends. A few chablis glasses later, I find myself retelling stories of a year in France playing Alec in the film *Tess*, directed by Roman Polanski, with my old friend Peter Firth as Angel and new friend Nastassja Kinski as Tess, which seemed to at once both amuse and terrify some of the younger ones. Another story to tell, but not now.

It's 3 am on the whatever it is, of whatever it is. Two shows tomorrow, or rather today. But a welcome nine hours' sleep before leaving for the theatre.

My advance schedule informs me I now have an appointment or two, six days a week in the theatre for the next nine months.

It's hard to let sleep be your master when your heart is beating this fast.

I'm on my school rugby pitch, or is it the set of our play? The field is planks of wood, painted rainbow colours. In the distance where the red bleeds into the luminosity of a star spangled midnight blue sky, I see the thin "H" shape of golden goal posts. I'm running fast up the field towards them, the rugby ball tucked under my arm, but it's not a ball, it's the moon. I'm dressed as William Shakespeare for the school play. Puck is a huge, blue-black ostrich or emu with bright yellow beak and mad blood-red eyes, chasing me, snapping at my heels, trying to bring me down. I throw the moon ball to the ground. It bounces high over the crossbar between the goalposts. Titania in her long pink ostrich feather dress is swinging on her swing, suspended from the "H" crossbar and being pushed by a floating Theseus to and fro, to and fro, laughing, laughing; I leap after the moon ball as it glides over her head and I become Oberon, flying through the goalposts trying to catch the moon, my huge sequinned cloak billowing behind me:

"Ill met by moonlight proud Titania,"

I cry to her as I fly by.

"What jealous Oberon?"

She replies laughing, laughing as golden-cloaked Theseus gives her swing another mighty push.

"We the globe can compass soon,
Swifter than the wandering moon."

I yell, beckoning her.

"Fairies skip hence,
I have forsworn his bed and company,"
She commands.

Fairies in wild yellow, red and blue ostrich feather wigs, form a scrum beneath her and she glides down into them and is enveloped like plankton into a sea anemone.

Purple cloak billowing, I fly toward the moon pursued by the blue-black demented emu snapping at my heels. The colours and figures in a Chagall painting. Disjointed dream images.

"When they next wake all this derision
    Shall seem a dream and fruitless vision..."

I chant as my arms reach out to grasp the moon. But it's not the moon; it's a gaudy brittle glass globe, a Christmas bauble, a decoration. As my trembling fingers touch it, it explodes like a bomb, shatters into a thousand shimmering shards and falls glittering into infinity in a cumulus cloud of vapour.

In horror and alarm, emu screeches, shrieks, screeches, shrieks, perforating my eardrum. I'm jolted into consciousness by the piercing somnambulistic screech of the telephone on the bedside table.

"Hello, my darling, how'd it go?"

"Uh, oh, hello, hello gorgeous."

"Hello, darling, did I wake you?"

"Oh hell, yeah. S'Okay, doesn't matter. Nice to hear your voice."

"How was First Night?"

"Umm, great, I'm told – I think."

"Don't you know?"

"Er, no. Not really. Adrian and everyone seem pleased. I think I remember the curtain call but I might have dreamt it."

"I bet you were great. I was thinking of you."

"I know you were, angel. Thanks for the flowers. How's Carolina?"

"I'm not in Carolina. I'm in Atlanta, Georgia."

"Atlanta! Why? What's happened?"

"There was a hurricane, haven't you seen the news?"

"No, not since you left."

"We've had a terrible hurricane. It was heading straight for Wilmington, Carolina, Connie Sellecca and I got in a car and just drove eight hours, four hundred miles."

"Are you safe there?"

"Yeah. We're fine, but all the locations were decimated in Wilmington today."

"So what's going to happen?"

"Don't know. We're waiting to hear, but we'll be at least a week behind schedule I'm told."

"Does that mean you won't be back for your birthday?"

"Probably. I'll push them as much as I can but I'll be back for our anniversary and your last night in London. I love you and miss you."

"Let me know as soon as you hear, I love you too."

"Take care of yourself, I'll call you tomorrow. Good luck with the show today. Have a bit more sleep."

"I'll try. Take care and tell 'em to hurry up, I want you home."

"Bye."

"Bye."

Click – burrr.

I make my way through the tragically ill-conceived Barbican complex to the stage door. The stage doorman, who in this case is a stage doorwoman, greets me in her usual gentle Irish manner.

"I hear it went well last night."

"Yeah, thanks, seem' to go okay."

I pick up a couple of late arriving First Night cards from the L to N pigeon hole, dump them in my dressing room and, not chancing what mood the hung-over lifts may be in after a First

Night, hop, skip and jump down the four flights of stairs to the
Green Room in the basement.

It's all a bit unreal. In the Green Room some of the company
are sitting around a table laughing, drinking coffee, smoking
cigarettes. Everyone is sunshiny beaming.

"Seen the reviews, Leigh?"

I'm handed the *Evening Standard*, de Jongh writes:

"The Barbican may be a nightmare to find, but the nightmare
turned into a dream to remember last night, classic theatre at its
best."

Michael Coveney in the *Guardian* writes:

"Beg, steal or borrow but don't miss this production of *A
Midsummer Night's Dream* superbly directed with a superlative
cast."

These are the sort of reviews an actor dreams of.

Which is precisely what I'm doing as the bedside alarm clock
shakes itself and me, for the second time tonight, into life.
Buzzing in my ear like a persistent wasp spoiling an otherwise
perfect picnic. It's the crack of noon. The morning after the
night before. It's been a hard day's night.

Some dreams disappear on waking, but last night's dreams
stay with me, vivid and clear, a confusing experience in the
subconscious theatre for one. Freud's theory was that dreams
could be roughly divided into fears and desires, that dreams
could be prompted by external stimuli – but were in effect wish
fulfilment rooted in our fancy, and held a serious meaning, but
what meaning? Discounting the phone call from Atlanta, still a
fitful morning/night's sleep suffused with subconscious images,
full of fears and desires Freud would have no doubt deduced.
The second dream is, I suppose, clearly desire. But why am
I dressed as William Shakespeare on a rugby field in the first
dream? I read there is a connection between dreams and the
area of the brain that produces creative art. For example, when
one looks at the work of Dali, Picasso, Chagall, the novels
of Gabriel García Márquez, the poetry of Ezra Pound or T

S Eliot, or even Coleridge amongst others, although his was helped along with a bit of opium. They all use symbolism in the way we use it in dreams. In theatre the conscious and subconscious are so interrelated they become almost meaningless without each other. Aristotle believed dreams were fragments of recollections of events of the day. And that to understand dreams one had to understand metaphor in which one image describes another. Centuries later Jung suggested that dreams are important messages from ourselves to ourselves, messages that we ignore to our loss, that although a difficult task dreams could and should, be interpreted, as dreams were meant to be understood. The Gestalt theory sees dreams as aids to the organisation of information, that the dreamer should consider every element of the dream which will relate to some unfinished business of the mind.

So why am I running up the rugby pitch that isn't really a rugby pitch dressed as William Shakespeare, for the school play?

Oberon, Theseus and I sit at the kitchen breakfast table, sip tea and munch on a muffin.

"I'm weary but contented," I say to Theseus and *zeeep* playback and there it is – well some of it. Last night's disrupted dream starts to fall comfortably and uncomfortably into place.

> "And send us to our resting beds weary but contented. Amen..."

is one of, if not the only, line of prayer I remember from the house assembly at school.

School assembly was an arse-achingly boring event of prayers, school announcements and hymns presided over by our house master, the black-robed, cane-wielding Mr Ellis, each morning before the horror of the academic day began. The rows of green-blazered boys, steeped from eleven-year-old midgets at the front to the frightening acne'd seventeen-year-old menboys at the back. I was in the middle. We were spied on from the side lines by Mr Butler and Mr Trollope. Trollope was a tall, cadaverous, scruffy teacher-type, ragged fringy moustache with dirty teeth, halitosis and a funny eye. He looked like Ben Turpin, the silent film comedian I'd seen at Saturday morning film shows at my local cinema, and I could hardly look him in the face without wanting to laugh. Not much danger to us, Trollope's sole concern at assembly seemed to centre around self-conscious attempts, during the hymn singing, at ensuring his foghorn basso-profundo descants would drown out the piping midgets at the front, and embarrassing octave-hopping boy-to-man sounds droning in discord from the back.

Butler, who taught Maths and Rugger, was a different teacher-type. Young, athletic, handsome-ish, patrolling the perimeter like a linesman.

Not understanding Maths, not being in the house rugger team, his interest in me stretched only as far as his obsession in ensuring my friend Ronal Shufflebottom and me were kept apart during assembly, to prevent us from diluting the boredom with whispered commentary on the housemaster's speech of the day, giggling at Trollope, and generally improving on the words of the prayers and hymns.

Butler would attempt to dismantle this creative force by the cunning device of ordering Shufflebottom or me to stand down front with the midgets for the rest of assembly, standing in humiliation, head and elbow above our giggling inferiors and singing a couple of testosterone octaves below them.

Not that I wanted to, but I believe the reason I didn't get into the house rugby team was because of my innovative strategy of psychological warfare I developed early in the game at the compulsory trials.

I had been positioned on the wing. At twelve years I was fast but very thin and quite small for my age. When running up the field with the ball safely tucked under my arm I was constantly thwarted by some big bugger who would hurl himself at my ankles and bring me down to fall on the rock-hard, slimy ball in the thick wet mud. I didn't like it. I liked it even less when jumped on by half a dozen louts and pummelled from all sides until the ball was inveigled from under me.

I quickly came to resent this so I developed a brilliant technique to protect myself from the pummellings and enable me to score a few tries. My psychological warfare took the form of, once in possession of the ball, streaking like hellfire up the field, making manic aggressive deep-throat growls and demented high-pitched howls, face twisted in menacing thin-lipped grimace, white-knuckled fist jerked back ready to strike anyone fool hardy enough to get within range. My mad Samurai warrior was obviously convincing because if any lout was foolhardy enough to come within a yard of me, from any direction, I switched from mad Samurai mode into berserk Samurai mode.

Without fail there would be a look of complete amazement and total fear that stopped even the biggest manboy from risking his life by getting any closer to the raving lunatic with the ball, leaving the way clear for me to streak up the field, and spectacularly dive behind the line for a touchdown.

I honestly thought this was brilliantly clever. I didn't break any rules because I didn't actually hit anyone, and as long as I could sustain the mad Samurai performance, no one would dare come near me, I could score some tries and modestly receive the awestruck congratulations and back-pats from my team mates.

No mud. No pummellings.

After a couple of successful runs culminating in more spectacular dives over the line, I was on my third Samurai charge when Butler, who was reffing, blew his whistle and disqualified me.

"Why, sir?"

"Disruptive behaviour, that's why."

"But, sir, how, sir? I haven't hit anyone, sir. I've broken no rules, sir. If they haven't got the bottle, sir, to tackle me, sir, I should be allowed to run with the ball, sir."

But he was determinedly closed to accepting any innovative techniques in rugby strategy from me, and I couldn't think of any other certain way to avoid the brain-juddering falls and rib-cracking pummelling that appeared an inevitability once robbed of my Samurai warrior characterisation. So, I played the rest of the game defensively, i.e. fumbled the ball and dropped it as soon as it came to me, or passed it like a hot coal from hell to a player on either team who didn't seem to mind a good pummelling. Broken noses, and collarbones, concussion and kicked-out teeth were, if not common, not rare.

So, at the risk of inevitable retribution from Mr Butler in morning assembly, I decided I would stay out of the house rugby team, and the hospital, and settle for a slightly less physically risky extra curriculum activity – in the house drama group. My first role was in a play called *The Rehearsal* by God-knows-who. It wasn't the innovative fifties play by Anouilh of the same title. This one took place at the first ever rehearsal of *Macbeth*, or "the Scottish play" as it is now referred to by the superstitious, which means just about anybody who makes their living in the theatre.

The characters were made up of Shakespeare's original company of players – Richard Burbage, Will Sly, Heminge, Fletcher, etc. I was cast as William Shakespeare. My costume was made at home by my mother, an excellent seamstress. A pair of my elder sister's baggy navy blue school knickers were commandeered and adorned with some pink silk strips cut from an old petticoat of my mother's and then stuffed with newspapers to make them blouson out. This gave a mysterious rustling sound to my every move, and left a peculiar flat collapsed look after rising from a sitting position. Thick lisle stockings, sister's again, held up by a garter belt, sister's; a white, cut-down blouse with a frill at the throat, mother's; paper doily ruff from the cake-making shelf that would leave angry red welts around my neck if I looked in any direction other than straight ahead. The image was completed with some crepe hair cut to make a moustache and goatee beard gummed onto my, as yet, razor-shy chin. It wasn't exactly Angels and Berman's Theatrical Costumiers standard that I was to get to know so well in later years, but far enough away from my hated usual school garb of green blazer and scratchy grey flannel shorts to make me feel like the man himself.

Until last night's dream, just about as far from a rugby field kit and Mr Butler as I thought I could get, and that suited me fine. I suspect the play wasn't very good either, but it gave me a first-hand, first-time introduction to Shakespeare with the lines –

> "Listen men, I've rewritten that speech and I think it
>   should go:
>   Tomorrow, and tomorrow, and tomorrow
>   Creeps in this petty pace from day to day
>   To the last syllable of recorded time
>   And all our yesterdays have lighted fools
>   The way to dusky death. Out, out, brief candle.
>   Life's but a walking shadow, a poor player
>   That struts and frets his hour upon the stage
>   And then is heard no more. It is a tale
>   Told by an idiot, full of sound and fury
>   Signifying nothing."

Still know them by heart. Still fill me with wonder as they did that long time past. Despite the costumes, we used somehow to regularly win the inter-house Drama Cup every year and there it was placed on the shelf, high up on the wall, alongside the Rugger Cup that they would sometimes miraculously win, despite the absence of my Samurai warrior. Polished and gleaming, the cups would stand gazing down on us at assembly to remind us of what an honour and how proud we should feel to belong to Spencer House. But fuck knows who Spencer was when he was at home. I never did find out.

Mine was the first intake in the great new experiment of comprehensive schools. The proven successful grammar school system that had given such a great start to so many working-class kids was for the most part scrapped or eased out and we were streamed into the comprehensive system according to our eleven-plus exam results. It was a miserable time for me and, but for Mr Twistleton, art teacher, and the extra curriculum pottery and art tuition, and for the escape of the drama group, I didn't fit in at all. I got the impression Art and Drama were not really considered in any way important in the great new scheme of things.

My dad bought me a pair of second-hand, full-size, peeling, brown leather boxing gloves from someone he met in a pub. He told me they had belonged to Joe Louis, the world champion. And I believed him.

He showed me a few moves, left hand up guarding the chin, right hand jabbing, dance, duck and weave. I'd shadow-box for hours on my own, or with him if he was drunk enough to bother but not so drunk he couldn't. I tried for the house boxing team, won a few bouts. But if my opponent got through my guard and bopped me, even lightly on the nose, it would pour with alarmingly bright red blood, streaming down my chest, staining my shorts. Didn't hurt and I would plead to go on, but Mr Butler the ref would stop the fight. So the gods and Mr Butler pushed my fate further towards the theatrical arena. Thank you gods. Thank you Mr Butler.

Mingled in the Freudian symbolism of desires and fears, I think I detect a gratifying un-Freudian trace of up yours Ellis, up yours Butler, up yours Trollope, up yours comprehensive school.

Oberon and Theseus try to convince me this explanation is an oversimplification of my dreams and that much more importance should be placed on their presence in them – but they would say that, wouldn't they?

How easy it is to be positive about just about everything when one has that feeling of right time, right place. When in love, the surety of knowing I'd rather be here now at this time, with this person, than anywhere else, at any other time, with anyone else in the world. I feel that love for this play, production and company. I feel no envy or regret when I read or hear who is shooting a movie in Hollywood. A film at Pinewood. Doing a TV series at Borehamwood. Or anyone else doing anything else in any other wood. I'm an *MND* junkie. My next fix is all I think about. Everything seems to relate to it. Everything I read, or hear. People I see or hear in the street, a voice, a walk, bring me back, remind me of my addiction. Happy or sad, waking or sleeping. Jungian, Freudian, Lawsonian psycho-biography of dreams when my head hits the pillow to sleep. A plethora of little inspirations everywhere I look when awake. Psycholytic therapy. This is my trip, I'm as hypnotised, happily mesmerised, as a magic mushroom on acid. Nothing offers more fulfilment or fulfils more promise of promise. Here we go again. The ordinary transcended, made unordinary.

SEVEN

Oberon, Theseus and I walk from the tube station through the Barbican high-rise cubes of concrete and slabbed nightmare wilderness of some architect's dream. We still get lost trying to find the theatre as have hundreds before us and will hundreds after us. I tell Oberon and Theseus I remember the bullshit spouted about this disfigurement by people who should know, or have learnt better, at the unfortunate time of its proposed construction. Those of us who did know, or had learnt better, were told we were ill-informed, retrospective-looking morons, frightened of change and progress. Our desperate voices of protest and disapproval dismissed with the arrogance borne of ulterior-motivated town planners and egocentric architects put on the planet to make the world a worse place to live in. Derided for refusing to deny what our eyes and ears, sentiments, instincts, education and history screamed out would be yet another architectural tragic travesty. Bad for now. Worse for the future. I saw it as a boy growing up in the Midlands. Perfidious pocket-lining bullrings and precincts tearing the heart out of our cities and countryside.

I feel the pollution scratching at my eyes, tightening on my lungs as we carve our way through the gruesomely sinister leaking concrete traffic tunnel that leads to the turning for the stage door. I curse the self-serving, untalented, profligate, dickheads who conceived and made their fortunes throwing up this disfigured prodigy. I know I have to try not to care. But I do care. I care so much it hurts. And I can't understand why everyone I pass doesn't say,

"Look what they've done, what they're doing, let's tell them it's got to stop."

"Calm, calm," says Theseus, "we have a play to do – twice."

The main stage in this theatre isn't a problem – once you find it. It's a comfortable space to play, and after a company voice class, held before each performance, I look forward to getting on there and starting the process of re-mapping my performance. Having got the horror of the First Night over, I know what I now must do. Despite the nice things said. The certain knowledge that I am only going to enjoy the journey and get the self-satisfaction I'm seeking if I go back to basics. Not quite, but almost start again. Keep some of what I've discovered, but re-examine what I've found. Re-evaluate it. Some things have by necessity been very rushed. I want to go back and look at every word, move, every thought. I'm feeling like I've missed breakfast and lunch and gone straight into dinner, sat down at a huge banquet in black tie and tails, and realised I've still got my pyjamas on underneath. I'm concerned a bit of striped pyjama may stick out below my trousers.

I know what I have to do. I know I have time to do it.

We've rehearsed back to front, we had to get a show this complex on in three and a half weeks. It must, as Adrian points out, remain a work in progress. I have much work to do. Oberon, Theseus and I are looking forward to the climb with great excitement and anticipation. A challenge to find some new routes up the mountain. Do a bit of abseiling, set up some base camps and find time to occasionally stop and look at the scenery.

*

> "Asking a working writer what he
> thinks about critics is like asking
> a lamp post what it thinks about
> dogs."
>
> *Christopher Hampton*

Some actors profess not to look at their reviews. Most that say they don't – do. I always say I do, but sometimes – don't. Unlikely as the chance may be there's always a remote possibility one may learn something. However remote that possibility usually I can't risk not taking that chance and having a glance. It doesn't matter, it's one person's opinion. I've seen perform-ances that it would appear by the reviews must have been great on First Night but have disappeared up the actor's jacksey by the time I get there. I've seen wonderful performances that have gone virtually undetected by the critical fraternity. I quite often disagree with what I read.

A critic at *The Times* reviewed Pinter's *Old Times* on our first night in Clwyd before we transferred to London last year. He took the trouble to come to Wales even though critics weren't invited. He made some points that I took on board and were a help. Maybe I would have found them anyway given time in performance, but in this case it helped me get there sooner. Problem being, although we were reviewed again in *The Times*, I don't think he personally came again when we opened in the West End to see the fruits of his and my labours. Anyway, much more important to me than any reviews of any kind was that Harold Pinter had suggested me for the part. By the time we were in the West End we had already gleaned some wonderful reviews for *Old Times*, but Harold telling me I was excellent as Deeley negated whatever any critic may have been moved to write, good or bad. It's often the money-men and producers who invest too much importance in a newspaper review.

Generally, actors know whether they are in something that works or not. But once in print, it is so final, quoted thereaf-ter. A run should, must, remain a voyage of discovery. Most critics see it in its embryonic state, but history will refer to their critiques for future generations. Maybe join in the dance later. Whatever they say, good, bad or indifferent, at the moment they can only get in my way and blur the image for me as I look ahead.

First Night was a bit on automatic pilot or like taking a driving test: I know I'm never going to drive like that again, too careful, too cautious. I suppose all we really want to see when the page is opened, or the review pinned on the noticeboard, is to read how incredibly, unbelievably wonderful we and our production are, and I've already had the luxury of reading that in the second half of last night's dream.

Second nights, famously a let-down after the euphoria of a First Night but surprisingly not so today. Two great shows, wonderful reception, six rewarding curtain calls. But I'm becoming very concerned about my voice. It's beginning to feel strained and tired.

Made some progress with the pyjamas.

A week becomes one long day with breaks for sleeping really only marking the time between performances. A routine, a strictly structured day. Light lunch or snack before, or on matinee days, between shows. Exercises, physical and vocal, part of the daily routine. Eat well, rest well, no alcohol before the show, judicious amount after. Arrive at the theatre at least an hour and a half before curtain up, everything geared to the performance. TV can now be watched in the evenings after the show, sometimes a panacea until the early hours whilst waiting to come down from the adrenaline rush. If no matinee next day, maybe to a restaurant with friends who come to see the show.

No doubt London is the place to be if you're in a successful play: you feel as if the town belongs to you, you have an indelible right to be here. You are a major part in its present importance. A part of its historical charm and contributor to its present allure. Parliament may close, bridges collapse, the Thames stagnate, restaurants close, banks go bankrupt, taxis go on strike, the airports close, TV stations blackout, the sex shops become churches and the churches strip clubs, and it wouldn't matter without you. No other elixir, with the exception of falling in love, has this effect on the senses. The world would stop revolving without your show.

I awake today with not exactly a pain in my throat, but a tension and slight swelling. Bypassed all other emotions and went straight to panic. I telephoned Neil Constable, our tour manager: very helpful, very very efficient. Within a short while I have a phone call to say I have an appointment to see Tim Harris, throat specialist, whose surgery is in Blackheath.

"Where the hell's Blackheath, for Christ's sake?" Sounds like Macbeth's weekend retreat.

"South East London," I'm told.

I knew it sounded ominous.

Several hours later, most of which have been spent travelling to Black-bloody-heath I'm with the cheerfully disposed Mr Harris. I sit in the reclining black leather chair in Tim Harris' surgery. He feeds a thin metal tube down my throat with a bright red light at its tip.

"Try not to swallow. This tube has a micro-camera on the end," he says.

I have no desire to swallow, I have a great desire to do the opposite. I gaze at the monitor over my head, watch what seems to be the replay of a BBC2 documentary demonstrating the conception process. The camera creeps along the vaginal passage and approaches the cervix.

"There we are," says Dr Harris. "Look at the monitor and you'll see clearly your vocal chords, a little mucus on them, a little red and inflamed."

"He hat hi hohal hors?" I gag.

"Yes, nothing seriously wrong."

"Ha hoo hor?"

"Yes, certain. No pharyngitis or laryngitis, no nodules."

"Hank hog."

A few minutes later when the cable TV has been retrieved from my throat, he tells me,

"Your chords are perfect, but you've been overworking them, stress and fatigue are playing a big part in this too. I see this a lot in my opera-singing patients when performing after travelling from Milan to New York, New York to London, London to Paris."

"Earls Court to Blackheath?" I ask.

He then embarks on a lengthy metaphor about athletes preparing for a big event and resting immediately afterwards. I'm afraid he left me behind at about the second hurdle.

Tim Harris is a pioneer in the study of the human voice. Instead of pumping the patient full of steroids and cortisone he believes in a technique of osteopathy and relaxing the muscles that suspend the voice box, or vocal chords, or cervix – depending on which film you're watching.

He recommends a course of treatment with an osteopath in Rotherhithe called Jacob Liebermann, known at the RSC as "The Rotherhithe Strangler".

An appointment is made for me.

"Where the hell's Rother-fucking-hithe, for Christ's sake?" You can tell the boy's done Shakespeare. "Is it on the banks of the Clyde?"

It might just as well be.

My emergency appointment is made for 9.30 am next day. My diagnosis has been given as suffering from fatigue and stress. Getting to Rother-fucking-hithe at this unearthly hour of the morning ain't going to help a whole lot. Got through the show but my voice was very weak by the end and my throat was swollen and throbbing. I'm very concerned but manage to stay just this side of panic.

The curtain came down at 10.30 pm. I'm home by 11.30 pm. An hour to eat and shower. Up at 6 am, three mugs of tea and two fucking hours on the train to fucking Rother-fucking-hithe.

Are you ready for this – ?

To be told I've got the wrong day, to come back same time tomorrow.

I want to scream but I can't – damage the voice.

Anyway, I decide it imprudent to hurl abuse at somebody known as the "Rotherhithe Strangler".

Too far to go all the way back home across London to face the inevitable barrage of daily phones and mountain of mail.

I feel as if I haven't slept in a fortnight. I drag my weary frustrated carcass to the theatre, throw myself on the settee in my dressing-room, throw some big Zs heavenward, each bearing a winged prayer to the voice god. "Please give me a voice tonight, please give me a voice tonight."

I awake in time to catch a matinee performance of *Faust* in the Pitt Theatre downstairs. Can it really only be four months since we did *The Relapse* in this Theatre? Seems like a lifetime ago.

Michael Feast is magnificent as Faust. For the first ten minutes as the old man I don't recognise my old friend. Vocally, physically, mentally, in every way he's someone else – he is Faust. A reward for a nightmare start to the day.

EIGHT

Michael Feast and I met as eager young actor laddies in 1970 in Italy.

We had both recently left drama school in London: Mickey, the Central School of Speech and Drama; me, the Royal Academy of Dramatic Art. We were to appear in our first film. It was the story of St Francis of Assisi to be called *Brother Sun, Sister Moon*, directed by Italian film maestro Franco Zeffirelli, who had already had huge acclaim and success with his films *Romeo and Juliet* and *Taming of the Shrew*. The film was to be shot in various parts of Southern Italy and Sicily. Originally a three-month shooting schedule, filming continued another seven months beyond that. Albeit about the life of St Francis of Assisi, there was very little spiritual about the experience.

It was a bizarre sequence of events that preceded my appearance in the film, and I was forced to take a ride on an emotional roller coaster of euphoria to despair, despair to resignation, back to euphoria, back to despair, back to resignation and so on until the ride ended. All this over a period of six months or so, before even starting work on the film.

A glimpse for a young actor at that time that was to serve as an invaluable insight into the devious, duplicitous nature of the movie-making machine, and some of those who grease its cogs and their palms.

It's the last year of the decade. 1969. The year of my graduation from the sometimes comfortable, sometimes not, but nevertheless safe, caring, brutal, brilliant, life-changing, Royal Academy of Dramatic Art.

On the whole, RADA had been a happy and certainly edifying experience. I came out with a couple of prizes, an agent, a job, and a great deal more sexual experience than I entered with.

Of the agents that had shown interest in representing the green young rookie, I chose, with my Principal Hugh Cruttwell's advice, an agent called Jimmy Fraser at a well-respected, medium-sized agency called Fraser and Dunlop.

To me, at that first meeting, Mr Fraser was a rather forbidding figure. A tall, fleshy Scotsman with a brick-red face, thick white hair, and as gay as a maypole. The job was at the Yvonne Arnaud Theatre in Guildford understudying George in *Who's Afraid of Virginia Woolf?*, and playing Jerry in *The Zoo Story*, both by Edward Albee. Two enormous parts that turned my brain to addled eggs in the learning. I vowed never to understudy again, and never did.

I'm sent to see Zeffirelli's casting director. He's a handsome young man, tall and worked out, blond hair, slightly South African accent. Looks like he could be an actor. Which is what he was, before the Maestro elevated him to the privileged status of being able to sit with his feet on his desk when other mere actors enter his office.

I enter his office.

He is reclining in a chair with his feet stretched out on the desk in front of him. Is this informal pose to put me at ease? Or intimidate me? I want to believe the former, but insecurity convinces me it's the latter.

The handsome hunk pulls furtively on an inverted cigarette palmed between his thumb and forefinger, looks over his fist and eyes me, reminiscent of a farmer deciding whether to bid on a sheep or cow at the once-weekly cattle market I used to visit as a young boy in Warwickshire.

So this is what a casting session's like. I'd heard them referred to as cattle-calls by other actors. I worry, are my horns curved enough? Too skinny, too fat? My eyes bright enough, teeth white enough? Is my hide thick enough as an actor or a bull?

I'm nervous and apprehensive. I know a successful bid from the farmer may result in a visit to the slaughterhouse, but pride dictates no bid means rejection. Rejection, the actor's arsenic. A large dose can kill you straight away – small doses, poison over a period of time.

The antidote?

"Sold to the furtive fag-smoking farmer with his feet on the desk."

Came the call from the tall camp Scotsman, my new agent Jimmy Fraser.

"Hello, Hen. You have an appointment to meet Franco Zeffirelli at Pinewood Studios for his new film, *Brother Sun, Sister Moon*. Smarten yourself up a bit, Hen, your hair looked a terrible mess last time I saw you. And wear your nice leather jacket."

"What, no udders and horns?" I ask.

"What d'ya mean, Hen?"

"Oh, never mind."

Discussions of hair and what to wear seem to take precedent over career planning with the Big Jock Jim, I'd noted. I'd been a student for two years, existing on ten pounds a week. I was broke. I liked scruffy. It was not only appropriate for a fledgling thespian, but unavoidable.

Franco Zeffirelli was famous. Infamous. I'd heard stories from other fledglings who'd worked on the Maestro's previous, hugely successful film, *Romeo and Juliet*. I didn't like what I heard. I was not impressed by the actor-embellished tales of the Maestro's *modus operandi*.

Leather-jacketed and hair brushed, I sit and chat to the friendly blond bombshell Casting Farmer – whilst the Maestro pentaxes my face from every angle, circling my seated figure of acute discomfiture – and try to pretend it isn't happening. The large, hollow Cyclops' eye shwoks a blink a few inches from my left ear, my right ear, three-quarter face, full face.

"'E 'as a good 'ead,' the Maestro says.

How does he know? I've hardly spoken.

"Cute noz, don yo' dink?" he says to the Farmer.

The Farmer exhales his ciggie smoke and smiles. A worrying smile.

Well, it worries me.

What about acting? Does acting figure at all in the equation? Is anyone interested in acting? Please, someone, mention acting – *can he act?*

"No, yo don' look a de camera pliz," says the Cyclops.

"Yo pretend it not there."

The Maestro is sophisticated Italian charm personified, though hardly the classic Mastroianni type. Potato-shaped head, thinning straight light brown hair swept back over his large cranium. Bright, intelligent blue eyes that frequently squeeze into a compulsive nervous blink, as if it's blurry and he has to clear his vision. A slight Tourette's twitch as if his shirt collar is too tight and he has to stretch his head leftward and give his neck a short sharp pull to release it from his collar.

He has a pleasing smile that shows a different side to the man, and I find myself imagining how he got the small scar that mars his lower lip. A punch from an actor? Or a lover? Or both?

He's very articulate, with a wide, heavily-accented vocabulary. Shirt cuffs turned back to reveal thin brown wrists, a fine gold chain on one and expensive gold watch on the other. A strong smell of Italian cologne. He smokes cigarettes like a forest fire, or is it Mount Etna waiting to erupt?

There's an undercurrent in the small room of something that makes me uneasy, unsure of myself, unsure of them. I'm aware, they're aware, I'm aware of this.

"And how much am I bid for this fine healthy young heifer? Six feet tall, weighs in at about 175 pounds, from good theatrical stock?"

"Hello, Hen, Franco wants you to do a film test," says my new best friend and agent, big Jock Jimmy Fraser, as I enter the door.

"Now, what would you like, Hen? I've this champagne left over from last night's party – I had a few friends round – or would you like wine, or something stronger? I'm having a whisky."

His flat is an expensive, unloved dump bachelor pad. Everything smacks of lonely.

"Can I use your toilet?"

"Aye, away and brush your hair. It looks terrible."

I return to a couple of hints on how to handle the film test, a couple of sips of flat champagne, a couple of lines of camp Scottish repartee. And I'm out of there on the tube, homeward bound, rehearsing in my head a speech I'd already learned from Christopher Hampton's play, *When Did You Last See My Mother?*, which I decide would suit admirably for the big day of the film test.

Later that night, the phone rings. It's Big Camp Jock Jim. He's pissed. I'd recognise a drunken Glaswegian if he were whispering from the top of Ben Nevis or the other end of Sauchiehall Street. I grew up listening to it: the Lawson name's as Glaswegian as the Gorbals.

I can't quite believe it but I think he's propositioning me, or sussing me, or pimping me.

"Now let me ask you this, Hen. Would you do anything" – "anything" is loaded – "to get on in this business?"

The message is implicit, clear. My response instinctive.

"Well, what do you mean by anything, Jimmy?"

"I mean *anything*, anything to succeed?"

"Erm, well, no, Jimmy. I'd like to think I can hang on to my integrity, such as it is, and succeed through whatever talent I may or may not have. But I certainly wouldn't do *anything*. But then I'm not expecting that will be asked of me."

"Uh, hu, that's what I thought, Hen," he mumbles. "Okay. Goodnight."

Cut, mix, dissolve, as they say in the world of movie-making I'm surely now about to enter.

I'm at Pinewood Studios at last, I'm given the number of a room to report to. I push open the door and enter to find the Maestro and a film crew pointing a camera at me.

THE DREAM

"Yo' jus' ac' naturel, yo' preten' da camera not 'ere."

I feel about as natural as a polar bear in the desert. I'm taken to another room and introduced to about half a dozen other young actor fledglings, of every type and variety. A German, a Swede, a tall blond American, a short dark American, and a couple of tall dark Brits. Apparently, Franco has been combing the entire globe to find his actor to play St Francis and his happy band of Franciscan Brothers.

"He's seen just about every English-speaking actor under thirty," I'm told by one of the fledglings.

The hot July sun beats down from a clear blue sky as we're led to a field of knee-length brown grass on the back lot behind the studios.

I'm led to the middle of the field. Three hundred yards away the Maestro and the camera are pointed in my direction, the camera crew look at my lonely figure as if I'm the round of drinks they'd been thinking about since breakfast.

"Okay. De camera is turning," the Maestro shouts through a cone-shaped loudhailer. "Yo' run toward de camera."

I run towards the camera.

"Now yo' stop."

I stop.

"Now yo' look down, oooh, der is a beautiful flower, God mad' dis beautiful flower."

I look down at dis beautiful flower God mad' in de imagination of dis actor.

"Now yo' run again toward de camera, yo' are so 'appy you' tek off your sheart. Yo' wave de sheart above your 'ead."

I'm so happy I take off my sheart?

I not understand what sort of 'appy dis is but do it anyway.

Now I'm skipping towards the camera and the puppeteer says,

"Now yo' drop'a to de groun'. Look up'a to de ski above you an' around yo' at de grasses, an' you' lov'a dem, becows God mad' all of dese dings."

And I drop to de groun' and look'a de beautiful ski above me, to de beautiful grasses around me dat God mad', that I now love.

And I silently say to de God in de ski dat mad' all dis' beautiful dings,

"Give me this fucking part or I swear I'll never speak to you again, dear."

"Now is lurnch," says the Maestro.

We go to lurnch.

The huge Pinewood Studio dining-room is wooden panelled. Buzzy, noisy, exciting in every way but the food way. "The wooden panelling comes from the disastrous wreck of a famous ship called The Mauritania," I'm told by one of the waitresses. I spot a couple of other wrecks of the non-nautical, silver screen variety, swigging wine, in make-up and costume of the current *Carry On...* film being shot there. The small dark Italian-looking American actor with us doesn't like his food and sits very quietly at the end of our long table. He's obviously here to test for the lead role of St Francis. I'm so hungry I could eat a horse, and might be, or it could possibly be a piece of the saddle.

But there's a contained thrill about being at the famous Pinewood Studios amongst the small band of possible happy brotherhood. One of the other British fledglings seems to be approaching the whole thing with a similar sense of humour to my own. He is obviously being tested for the same part as I am. We are both aware of this and, bonded in adversity, pledge to telephone the other as soon as one or other hears if they have the part.

Blond Bombshell Casting Farmer arrives and through inhalations on a furtive fag asks us to think of a song: Franco has decided we should each sing as part of the film test. A guitarist has been hired to come in and accompany us. Apparently the happy band of foundling Franciscan Brotherhood used to wander the medieval streets of Assisi, in all weathers, singing medieval songs in an attempt to convince the irritated locals to give up their lives of medieval comfort, give away their possessions, have their heads shaved, wear sackcloth robes, go barefoot, beg for food, and bathe a few sores at the local leper colony. Well, how could such an appealing proposition fail to find favour and attract a following? But it did, the young people of the town flocked to join this new cult of twelfth-century Christian Hari Krishnas.

We are taken to a room to practise our singing with the bewildered but enviably talented guitarist who had been found and hired for the ordeal an hour earlier. I decide to do a typically cheerful little dirge by Leonard Cohen called "I Love You In The Morning". The nervous fingers of the guitarist have trouble with the transition in the third verse. We try again. Nervous fingers pluck the wrong chords again.

"Why don't you just stay silent in that bit and come in again when it's over?" I suggest.

But professional pride piqued, he's determined to try and play the whole ditty.

By now, my entire being has about as much confidence in the song as the guitarist's plucking fingers.

At around this point the small, dark Italian-looking American, sitting simmering quietly in the corner, rises and strides to the door and says to Blond Bombshell Casting Farmer,

"Listen I'm a fucking actor, not a fucking singer. I've had enough of this, I'm outta' here. I'm going home."

And he leaves.

Blond Bombshell and the rest of us are aghast, flabber-a-ghast. Bombshell lights another ciggie from the stub of his last one.

What a fool. What an idiot. What confidence. For a young unknown actor to pass, to walk out on the possibility of playing the lead in the next smash hit film by the Italian Maestro is foolhardy, to say the least. This seems to be the general feeling amongst the remaining fledglings. Secretly tinged with a sliver of admiration for the courage of the man.

But with an attitude like that we all agree we'll never hear of him again.

"What's his name?" asks a fledgling.

Bombshell looks at his list.

"Um, Al something... Pacino, Al Pacino," says Bombshell.

Feeling like an unarmed gladiator about to face the lions, I'm led to the arena of the studio to do my song. There's a small, wooden rostrum surrounded by a big Panasonic camera, microphones, and blinding lights that the crew refer to as "Brutes, Blondes, Redheads" and other coded names with the familiarity of someone they meet regularly in the pub at lunchtime.

The Maestro introduces me to his Italian lighting cameraman, known as the DP. Director of Photography. Tall, built like a pizza oven, thick curly black hair, thick curly black beard, thick curly fat fingers. The thick curly fat fingers pincer and squeeze the left cheek of my face between thumb and forefinger – just a bit too hard – forcing my mouth into a Francis Bacon smile. He purses his lips and makes effusive Italian guttural sounds in his throat.

I feel like a new mule on a farm in Tuscany.

When the guttural sounds abate, a beaming pizza-oven smile and a sharp slap on the cheek – just a bit too hard.

No other nation can get away with this form of greeting – only the Italians. Only an Italian, by way of affectionate first greeting, can squeeze your cheek – just a bit too hard – slap your face – just a bit too hard – and get away without a reciprocal smack in the kisser – just.

I am about to do my first film test at the famous Pinewood Studios. Home of so many iconic classic British movies. But it's all foreign and weird to me. The British camera crew are speaking in strange coded terms, the Italians are throwing their arms around and don't seem to agree on anything. More importantly, the guitarist can't play the third verse of the song I now have to sing.

I sing the first two verses, stop, say, "That's all I know." Guitarist piqued – face saved.

I mount the rostrum to do my acting piece from *When Did You Last See My Mother?* by Christopher Hampton. I love this piece. I can identify with it. It starts wittily and becomes pensive, sad. I've joined two separate speeches together to make one.

On the spur of the moment I change "Mother" to "Father". Now the piece seems even more pertinent to me, I hadn't seen my own father for ten years. I finish, I have tears in my eyes. The Maestro approaches the rostrum, he has tears in his eyes. The hairy DP approaches, pincers outstretched. I cower back. He has tears in his eyes. The Maestro warmly shakes my hand.

"Det wos' wonderful. Dare is a part for yo' in my film, yo' will 'ear from us soon," he says gently.

Wings on heels I fly home.

"You did very well, Hen, Franco liked you a lot," says Big Jock Jim from behind his office desk. "But it'll be some time before filming starts."

"How long?"

"I don't know, Hen. I'll let you know. Now away and brush your hair, you look tired, have you shaved today?"

Cut! Mix! Dissolve! It's three days after the film test. It's the 21st of July. It's my birthday. In the morning I do an audition for the coming season at the Belgrade Theatre in Coventry.

The audition over, I chat to the laconic, somewhat distracted Welshman who is artistic director of the theatre.

"It's my birthday today," I tell him.

"I may have a birthday present for you, Boyo. Leave your home number. I'll ring you tonight."

I meet my delicious Turkish Delight girlfriend for lunch at Cranks health food restaurant, recently opened near where

Deliciousness works in the new trendy area of London called Carnaby Street.

As we walk, the Beatles' new album *Sergeant Pepper* surges and rushes out of the doorway of the shops and boutiques that line Carnaby Street and the lanes that lead off into the new London of the Swinging Sixties, and Cool Britannia.

Deliciousness and I stand at the counter in Cranks deliberating over the wholewheat apple crumble in the earthenware dishes, and turn to see the tall blond Casting Farmer sucking on a ciggie staring over his fist at the beanshoots and salad.

"You did very well," he says. "Franco wants you to play the part of Barnardo."

"Thank you. That's great. Is it a good part?"

"Very – one of the leads."

"Can I see the script?"

"Not at the moment, it isn't finished yet."

"It's my birthday today."

"Happy birthday."

Lady Fate often arranges a little surprise present for me around this time. On this same day three years ago I was offered a place at RADA. The wings on my heels that emerged that day, the ability to move without my feet touching the ground returns.

I aviate along Carnaby Street with Deliciousness on my arm. Clark Kent and Lois Lane window-shopping. Past flared trousers, mini-skirts, platform shoes, kaftans, Afghan coats, the smell of hash and joss sticks.

"Sergeant Pepper's Lonely Hearts Club Band", "Lucy in the Sky with Diamonds", "When I'm Sixty-four", "With a Little Help from my Friends", "Lovely Rita".

Lovely London. Lovely Deliciousness on my arm. Lovely Casting Farmer person. Lovely Franco Zeffirelli director person. Lovely cheek-squeezing Italian lighting man person. Lovely birthday.

Lovely phone call when I glide home from the lovely distracted Welshman I'd auditioned for that morning offering me a season at the Belgrade Repertory Theatre, Coventry, with a clause that I can be released at a month's notice at any time during the season, to enable me to start work on the Zeffirelli movie.

"Thank you," I say. "It's my birthday today."

"I know, Boyo. You told me. Happy birthday."

NINE

"The man who glories in his luck
May be overthrown by destiny."
Euripides

It's when the roller coaster starts its descent, gathers speed and falls faster and faster, that's when you wish to Christ you'd never got on, feel sick, feel scared, want to scream, want to get off.

Cut! Mix! Dissolve! And the chances I'll be hearing that phrase on a film set seem to be getting remoter by the month, the week, the day. It's now two and a half months since I've been nesting with four other young actor fledglings in a small house in Coventry. We are paid £10.10s a week by the theatre, except for one actor who's on £14 a week. We pay £2 each a week rent. When I haven't a shilling for the gas fire in my room I go to bed to keep warm and learn my lines. I don't care I haven't got enough money to eat. I'm a professional actor working in the theatre, a dream come true. Anyway, any day now the call will come and I'll be making a film in Italy. Every Wednesday night, the day before pay day, John Rhys-Davies, the actor who is earning £14 a week, generously stands us all the price of a bag of potatoes, a bob for the gas fire, and a pint of milk and some butter, and we sit around the gas fire in my room until the shilling runs out. No feel of romantic artists suffering for their art: just a resigned acceptance that one should expect no more if you choose to pursue your dream in the theatre. But what of the other dream?

What of the promised dream of acting in a film in Italy directed by the Maestro, Franco Zeffirelli? Earning some money, Italian sunshine, spaghetti Bolognese and a bottle of wine?

We sit around the fire sipping our milk, scoffing our truly delicious spuds, and one of the company tells me he'd read in the newspaper that filming had started on Zeffirelli's new big movie

Brother Sun, Sister Moon, in Italy. Alec Guinness is playing the Pope, he says. I'm shocked, scared and embarrassed.

Next day, pay day, I use precious shillings to phone Big Jock Jimmy, my agent who's pledged to looking after my career.

He's evasive, dismissive. The worm turns. But confirms:

Someone else is playing my part in the film.

I wonder if courage is lacking in the man; if so, surely professional courtesy should have dictated a call.

When challenged he replies:

"This is your testing time, Hen. You have to be resilient in this business, take a slap in the face and come up smiling."

I feel foolish, ignored, betrayed. But by who? How? I can scarcely believe what I'm hearing.

"Who looks after this actor playing my part?" I ask.

"Well, it's a wee bit embarrassing, Hen – but I do."

McHiavelli is a Scotsman. He's a theatrical agent, now living in London under the assumed name of "Jimmy Fraser".

Fuck you, Jimmy, fuck, fucky, fuck, fucking Machia-fucking-vellian Fraser. Fuck you Franco, fucky, fuck, fucking Zeffi-fucking-relli.

No wings on heels. His worn-out shoes are made of lead that lock onto the magnets concealed beneath the paving stones as he slopes away from the phone box to the theatre.

Rejection, the actors' arsenic. I swallow my dose. If taken in regular small doses one can build up a resistance to arsenic. It doesn't seem to be working for me. Perhaps the doses being pushed down my throat are too large too soon. The season I'd been engaged for draws to a close. I've had the opportunity to play some wonderful parts in the three-weekly repertory. I'm asked to extend my contract for a few more plays with the heady increase in salary to £12 a week. I agree, and complete the engagement. A good friend, the television writer/producer Wilfred Greatorex, whom I had known since before RADA, comes to see me in one of the plays: *The Hostage* by Brendan

Behan, in which I'm playing the 19-year-old British soldier. He offers me a part in an episode of his new TV series. Both his most recent TV series, *The Power Game*, and his feature film, *The Battle of Britain*, had been hugely acclaimed.

Back in London, I hear on the theatrical grapevine that the actor cast in my part in the movie has been fired, sacked, let go. Zeffirelli decided he didn't like him after all. I feel sorry for the poor bugger. A killer dose of arsenic for any young actor. Worse than not getting the part in the first place. I wonder, should I deny them further humiliation, give myself the satisfaction, and tell them to stuff it when they finally come back to offer me the part?

But the opportunity for this masochistic indulgence is denied me. Because they don't.

Then, another large dose of arsenic.

I ring Jimmy McHiavelli to tell him about the TV part. He doesn't mention the film.

"I hear the latest actor playing Barnardo has also been fired, Jimmy,' I say.

"Um. That's right, Hen."

Silence.

"What's happening?"

McHiavelli tells me the part has already been re-cast and is now being played by the fellow fledgling I did the film test with. The one that had become a mate that day, the one that had pledged we would call each other, whoever got the part.

A small betrayal but I'm raw, a small betrayal grows in proportion when betrayal is all around.

A sword in the flesh.

But who to trust?

"Who's his agent?" I ask.

"Um, I am, Hen."

Mysterium Tremendum

> "There is in the worst of fortune
> The best of chances for a happy
> change."
>
> *Euripides*

Time passes. I do the TV play, a wonderful part written for me by my friend Wilfred. A much-needed boost to my crumbling confidence in my survival, let alone my future as an actor.

Now, an unwanted lesson in lying, double-dealing and mystifying duplicity that the original Machiavelli would have been proud to have orchestrated himself, even if only for a bit of fun on a quiet day. I hear him even now, clawing on the lid of his Florentine tomb, angry at having to delegate to his twentieth-century disciples.

What takes place now all happens within the time-span of a week.

Out of the blue, or is it the black, I'm asked to go to a photographer's studio and see the Casting Farmer who has returned from Italy to cast the part of "The Leper".

I'm out of work. I'm broke. I feel like a leper. Might as well play one.

Jimmy McHiavelli tells me "The Leper" is a new major role, but I won't find it in the script because it isn't written yet. One or two other actors of a suspiciously similar type to me loiter around the ante-room to the studio. Casting Farmer is very kind: I think I sense slight embarrassment, I know I sense irritation at the position he has been placed in. I know how he feels. The feeling is mutual. I'm photographed from every angle again. Two days later Jimmy McHiavelli calls.

"They want you in Rome tomorrow, Hen. Take enough clothes for three days or three months."

"What does that mean, 'three days or three months'?"

"You'll be doing a film test when you get there, Hen, if after that they offer you the part, it's three months, if they don't, you'll be back in three days. Your ticket's on its way, you'll be met at the airport in Rome. Good Luck, Hen."

TEN

Rome is full of Italians. One of them is my driver sent to meet me at the airport. He holds up a piece of card with a name resembling mine on it. I can't understand a word he says. His expressive Italianate hand and face gestures let me know we're in for a long drive.

Two hours later we draw up outside a disproportionately large church in a small village somewhere in Tuscany. The usual paraphernalia of film-making is littered around the churchyard, spewed out by the huge articulated trucks parked nearby: lights, screens, ladders, dollies, flags. Thick black electric cables snake their way into the ancient church from the huge generator van that hums a tuneless hymn in the churchyard. I stand in front of the enormous church, suitcase in hand, feeling like a Lithuanian refugee on Ellis Island.

The Italians all speak at once, throw their arms about, laugh, slap each other on the back, pinch a few cheeks, slap one or two, and laugh their way along the snake-tracks into the church. A few moments later my driver appears, arm around Casting Farmer, Italian-style. Casting Farmer leads me to the church; about fifty yards ahead I catch sight of the Maestro's broad pate in the garish light, directing a scene in the corner of the medieval gothic nave.

I'm quickly hustled to the ancient stone steps that weave their way down into the vaults. The vaults are a hive of busy Italian bees. A hair and make-up section, wardrobe area, space for props and armour, costume department, production office.

"When they've finished shooting the scene upstairs, we'll do your film test," Casting Farmer informs me.

Hamlet or Nothing

"It is a great piece of skill
    To know how to guide your luck
    Even while waiting for it."
                                        Baltasar Gracian

I sit in the hair and make-up department. My jaw-bordering sideboards are shaven, my shoulder-length hair is cut short. The dedicated make-up man spends an hour and a half meticulously attaching a three-day, quarter-inch stubble to my chin and cheeks. Casting Farmer reappears.

"Do you know any *Henry V* by heart?"

"No. Why?"

"Franco wants you to do a piece from *Henry V*."

"But I've got a piece ready, I've worked on a piece for him."

Casting Farmer disappears and reappears a few minutes later with a Complete Works of Shakespeare. We're in a small village in Italy? I'm impressed. The book is open at *Henry V* as he hands it to me.

"What's this?"

"Franco would like you to do this speech from *Henry V* for your film test."

I glance down at the book. Act Three, Scene One:

"Once more unto the breech, dear friends once more:
    Or close the wall up with our English dead..."

"Listen, I can't learn this in an hour but I recently played Hamlet, let me have a look and recap and tell Franco I'll do Hamlet for him."

"Franco wants you to do Henry V."

"Tell him I'll do Hamlet or nothing."

Makeup finished and not a lepric sore in sight. A leper without a sore?

I'm taken to the costume department. I'm draped in chain-mail and leather tunic, a sword-belt and sword hung around my waist.

A leper in chain-mail and leather tunic with a sword? What happens if he draws his sword and his arm drops off?

I'm asked to wear a framed leather cowl over my shoulders, the rigid neck of which rises up under my chin like a twelfth-century surgical collar. Perhaps I'm to play a leper with whiplash? My head looks like a champagne cork ready to pop out of its bottle. I'm tired, I'm nervous. I'm in a bit of a don't-fuck-about-with-me mood.

"I can't act in this," I tell Casting Farmer.

"Franco designed it. He wants you to wear it," says Casting Farmer who, since I arrived must have sucked his way through an entire pack of Marlboros.

"I don't care if he made it himself, tell him I don't want to wear it."

I sit around and wait and study my *Hamlet* text. I'm taken to a large, musky-smelling, stone-pillared cellar that leads off down deeper into the bowels of the vaults. The camera crew are arranging the Brutes, Blondes and Redhead lights for my film test.

Eventually, the Maestro enters the room. He has an air of a monarch concerned about the state of his kingdom. His manner is rather diffident towards this prospective new subject.

Is it to mask his embarrassment at having to face me again?

Possibly. Possibly not.

Is it because the stroppy young actor won't do Henry V or wear the costume he's designed?

Possibly. Possibly not.

"Well, Mr Lowson," he says very slowly.

Is this a greeting?

"So, yo' don' do de spich I ask you?"

"No. I think it's unfair to ask me to learn a new speech in an hour and do it to the standard you'll expect of me and I expect of myself."

"An' yo' don' like de costumes?"

"It's not a case of don't like it. I couldn't move my head in it."

I think of the poor buggers who got the sack playing my part previously. If they had to try and act in a similar neck-brace no wonder it ended in a British Airways return flight.

"Okay. Lay Lowson. Let's see what you can do," says the kindless monarch.

"And turn over," says the First Assistant.

The camera turns.

"Speed," shouts the Sound Man.

"Action, " says the Maestro.

I lean against the stone pillar in the centre of the vault and begin my favourite Hamlet soliloquy.

I'm in just the right mood for this.

Oh what a rogue and peasant slave am I!	Oh what a rogue and peasant slave am I!
	To put up with this crap
Is it not monstrous that this player here,	Is it not monstrous that this player here
But in a fiction, in a dream of passion...	Placed in a fiction, caught in his dream of passion...
Who calls me villain, breaks my pate across	Who thinks me cattle, Pentaxes my pate across
Plucks off my beard and blows it in my face,	Sticks on a beard, slaps me in the face
Tweaks me by the nose, gives me the lie i'th' throat	Tweaks me on the cheek, gives me the lie i'th'throat

As deep as to the lungs –	As deep as to the lungs –
who does me this?	who does me this?
... Bloody bawdy villain!	... Bloody bawdy villain!
Remorseless, treacherous,	Remorseless, treacherous,
lecherous, kindless, villain!	lecherous, kindless, villain!

... And so on.

I've no idea how that went. The mood seemed right. The director didn't stop me.

One take. Finish.

Dovè La Luce

Fourteen hours ago I was in England. It's bizarre to be now standing in the vaults of a church in the middle of Italy's long leg doing yet another film test for the movie they are already shooting in the church above me.

It's been a long day. I'm glad it's over.

But is it? I'm led back into the wardrobe department in the vaults and change back into civvies. Then into the make-up department to take off my chin stubble and make-up. As I wipe the grease off my face, Casting Farmer appears, opening a fresh pack of Marlboro.

"What happens now?" I ask.

"We'll put you up in a hotel," says Casting Farmer.

"Where are you all staying?"

"You're not staying at the same hotel as us."

"Why not?"

"I'll tell you when we get outside."

He's nervous, his cigarettes are transmogrifying into ash as if he's smoking for Italy or England or South Africa or all of 'em.

"There's a problem," he says at last.

"Surprise me," I reply.

"I've been told to ask if you'd mind having a blanket thrown over your head when we go back through the church upstairs."

"You've been told what?" I ask with incredulity – though "incredulity" falls short of the astonishment and absurdly astounding, implausible, preposterous, exasperating, outraged, indignation that churns around my stomach and ennuied brain when I realise he's actually serious.

I can't get my head around this one, and things are certainly not going to be clarified by covering it with a blanket.

"But *why*?" I mouth.

"I'll explain outside."

Outside? Why outside? What does he have in mind? Fisticuffs?

"So do you mind doing that? Having a blanket over your head, and I'll lead you up the stairs and out through the church."

"Yes, I fucking mind. I mind very fucking much."

Visions of criminals with blankets over their heads, hustled from the police car into the court room zap between my unbelieving ears.

Paranoia.

Was my film test so bad they're ashamed if I'm even seen there?

Or perhaps the Maestro can't now bear to even see my face again?

"Please, as a favour to me," the agitated Casting Farmer asks.

"Abso-fucking-lutely not."

He disappears for three minutes.

"I'd like to go now," I say on his return. "And no blanket."

"No blanket," he replies.

When I get to the top of the stairs that lead up from the vault into the church nave, suddenly everywhere is plunged into total darkness. It's night outside and someone has pulled the plug on the lights inside. It's as black as the devil's mouth.

Casting Farmer miraculously produces a flashlight, takes my arm and leads me along the prayer-sodden pews and snaking cables through the black cavernous church and out of the huge ancient parched wooden doors. Behind me, excited Italian voices shout like children in a playground.

"Che fai?"

"Che cosa è?"

"Cosa succede?"

"Dovè la luce?"

The huge doors bang shut.

That was an efficient little operation. I'm a bit impressed. Couldn't get a blanket over my head so pulled the plugs! This is quite exciting now. What the fuck is going on?

I stand outside the church with a contrite Casting Farmer.

I'm calm. Confused. Dazed. But calm.

"Okay. Listen. Why don't you just tell me all about it. What's going on?" I ask, like a kindly priest in the confessional.

But it's gonna take more than three Hail Marys and a skip through the rosary for Absolution on this one.

The stone gargoyles on the pillars around the door of the church join me in wide-eyed, opened mouthed wonder as the story unfolds.

There is no major part of a Leper that I've flown out to film test for. The part doesn't exist. Never did. Never will.

I'm here to test, yet again, for the part originally promised to me, the part of St Barnardo. The first Barnardo replacement has already been sacked and returned to England, and I'm here because they want to do the same to the second.

But they can't sack him yet in case I don't get the seal of approval from Hollywood, where my film test is to be sent for a "Yes" or a "No" from the Paramount studio heads.

Hence, "Bring enough clothes for three days or three months, Hen".

Replacement Two wasn't scheduled for filming today so that I could appear and do my film test. But Replacement Two decided to make a surprise visit to the set to watch filming.

I was asked to put a blanket over my head so that Replacement Two wouldn't see me, and recognise me from our film test together at Pinewood.

When I refused, the lights were pulled by arrangement with the lighting crew so that I could be secreted out of the church unseen by their unexpected visitor, Replacement Two.

It's common knowledge to cast and crew that Replacement Two is probably for the chop. Common knowledge, that is, to all except Replacement Two. Replacement Two can't understand why the schedule has been changed and he isn't called for filming for the next week.

But they don't want to waste the time and money shooting on him, sack him, and have to shoot it all again on Replacement Three – if they find a Replacement Three.

I get the impression, if I'm deemed not suitable as Replacement Three, they'll stick with Replacement Two – that's why they're not telling him.

I can't imagine how cast and crew must feel forced into being a part of the conspiracy. But I discover others have already taken, and others will at a future date be taking, a British Airways return flight rather sooner than they expected.

Now, by implication, I'm part of the conspiracy. I ask Casting Farmer if I can see Replacement Two before either he or I are returned to England. We had a deal all those months ago that we would let each other know. He didn't keep his half of the deal but I want to keep mine. My request is refused on the grounds that he might get punchy. I argue that I think that an unlikely scenario, and will take the risk.

I'm told I'm being hidden in a hotel in town called Perugia, about an hour's drive away.

They finish shooting at this location today and move north to a new location in the mountains. I'm to wait in Perugia. I'm given some Italian Lire *per diem* for food.

"I always get the shit to deal with," says Casting Farmer.

But at least I've found someone to tell me, more or less, some of the plot so far and I get the impression he's trying to be as honest with me as possible. And I'm grateful for that small mercy. I'm uneasy about it but at least I know what shits I'm dealing with.

Or do I?

ELEVEN

"Ciao, ciao, Bambino" was the title of a popular song when I was a young boy. It's the only Italian I know: it means, "Goodbye, Baby", or is it "Hello, Baby"? – Anyway, not a lot of use when stranded on your own in a strange town in the middle of Italy. Unless you really want to get into trouble. Or, I suppose, get lucky. But I am in the mood for neither.

When the driver drops me at the hotel in Perugia I hand and face gesture I would like the telephone number of the production office. He scribbles a number on a piece of paper and drives off into the night.

It's an unnerving experience being alone in a foreign town, knowing no one, and not daring to go into a bar or restaurant, because you're not sure if you would be saying "Hello, Baby" or "Goodbye, Baby" to the bartender or waiter.

The only restaurant I can eat in is in the hotel where my smattering of French can be understood.

"For Christ's sake, speak English," I scream at the television in my room at regular five-minute intervals.

"Please, somebody, say something in Angleterra."

Breakfast, lunch and dinner alone in the hotel. A map and useless phrase book, a small amount of money in denominations that insist on remaining a mystery to me. After two wrist-slashingly lonely days pacing my hotel room, talking and arguing with myself and cursing every Italian gesticulating at me from the TV screen, there is still no phone call, no contact from the production.

Third day, I pack my bags and ring the number given me by the driver.

I get someone who speaks a sort of English, I tell him who I am and where I am, but much confusion over the name of the town I'm in. He seems confused as to where I am and who I want to speak to.

Have I been sent here and forgotten entirely?

He has a right to be confused. I don't know who I want to speak to either, I just want someone, anyone, to tell me what's happening.

Tell me I haven't been forgotten.

Tell me I can go home.

"Yo' wan' spek' signio Perugia?"

"What? No. I'm not Signor Perugia, I'm in Perugia. I want to speak to someone in Production, Produzione. I'm in Perugia and I want to speak to Produzione Office s'il vous plaît."

"Si, I get Signor Perugia."

"No, I'm not ringing to speak to anyone called Perugia. S'il vous plaît understandi, I'm calling from a town, a ville, in Italy, in Italia, called Perugia."

I'm on an Italian telephone merry-go-round but I ain't merry and I don't want to go round. I want to go home.

"'Ello, Lay. I am Signor Perugia."

Oh Christ.

"Listen, I didn't ask for you. I didn't ask to speak to Signor Perugia, I'm in Perugia. I'm an actor. My name is Leigh Lawson."

I'm interrupted by the voice on the phone

"Si. Is a liddle bit confusion, Lay. My name is Perugia, de sam' as de town yo' stay in. I'm a' de producer a' de film."

God, this is a confusing country. Why do they have to have a producer with the name of a town and why the name of a town they put me to stay in?

"Can you tell me what's happening, please, Mr Perugia? I've been here for three days, no one has contacted me. I want to know what's going on."

"I'm sorry for dis, Leigh, but I 'ave-a to tell yo', yo' 'ave gotta' depart."

I swallow my dose of arsenic. I'm disappointed but more pissed off.

"So why didn't someone call me? I've been in this fork-bendingly boring town, alone for three days. My bags are packed,

I'd like a car now, please, and I mean now, and I want the first possible flight home today, and I mean today."

More confusion from Mr Perugia on the end of the phone.

"No, no, Lay. Yo' don' understan' what I say. I say again for yo'. I am 'abbey to tell yo', yo' 'ave gotta' de part."

A long, Anglo-Italian silence.

Gotta' de part, gotta' the part, got the part, I have got the part.

"Oh, I see. I thought you meant depart, gotta' depart."

"Si, yes, yo' 'ave gotta' depart, we pick yo' up today, yo' come to de location for costume fittin' an' start filmin' in two days. I 'ope yo' 'ave hot clothes, is very cold and snowing 'ere."

But the gilt was scraped off the gingerbread months ago. It's not the pure thrill of a dream come true because of the nefarious torturous route to at last have the chance to stand in front of the camera and claim the part that had my name on it a long and winding road ago.

When I do my sums I realise a working-class lad's dream: I can afford to buy a house on completion of the film. The little wings sprout on my heels again and the streets of Perugia don't appear as lonely anymore, and the Italians are really very nice, and I'll soon pick up the lingo, I'll get used to the money.

I'm an actor playing a lead part in a Zeffirelli movie. I'm earning a living – I've proved I can do it, I'm beginning to be successful in a world that seemed a Utopian dream two years ago.

There's a book in the story of the ensuing ten months that I worked on the film but this is neither the time nor place for it. In that ten-month apprenticeship I learned about the craft of film-making. I learned from the Maestro and the people around him. Casting Farmer became a friend; so did the other fledglings playing St Francis and the Brothers, FIAs – Friends In Adversity. We all became very close, as one does in a film or a play when your fortunes and dreams are cast onto the same treacherous seas.

A quarter of a century has got behind us. Some of the Happy Band of Brotherhood have disappeared from my life for one reason or another. A few remain friends. Some seem to have disappeared from the acting profession altogether. The fledgling eventually chosen to play St Francis chose to commit suicide some time later, I'm told.

One of the Brothers, also making his first film appearance, was Michael Feast – the friend I saw being brilliant today as Faust in the RSC's Pit Theatre.

Now, in two separate plays, two of the young fledglings are playing the lead roles in a company revered the world over. We survived. We survive.

Author's collection

Top: The Relapse: On the right, with Michael Gardiner (front), Christopher Godwin (back) and Victor Spinetti in our one-bed dressing room.

Bottom: Second from right on the back row, with the rest of the cast of Peter Gill's Riverside production of *The Cherry Orchard*.

—— I ——

Author's collection

Left: With Dee Hoty, Denise Yaney, Bobby Cannavale and Bebe Neuwirth backstage at the Bay Street Theatre.

Below: As Sir Hugo, with Bobby as the waiter, in *Song at Twilight.*

Bottom: With Twiggy in New York.

Opposite, top: As Deeley, with Julie Christie as Kate, in *Old Times.*

Opposite, bottom: With Julie and Harriet Walter outside Wyndham's Theatre, London.

Photographer unknown

Alan Markfield

Photographer unknown

Author's collection

Author's collection

Brian Aris

Brian Aris

Above, top left: With Mickey Feast (fresh from *Faust*), backstage at the Barbican.

Above, top right: As Barnardo in *Brother Sun, Sister Moon*.

Above, bottom: The Brothers (Peter Firth, LL, Graham Faulkner and Michael Feast), with Alec Guinness as the Pope, in *Brother Sun, Sister Moon*.

Opposite, top: The Brothers with Franco Zeffirelli and his beloved loudhailer.

Opposite, bottom: Franco with his Director of Photography in pincer mode.

Brian Aris

Brian Aris

Donald Cooper

Clive Barda / ArenaPal

Clive Barda / ArenaPal

Clive Barda / ArenaPal

Opposite, top: The Lovers' scene in *The Dream*: LL as Oberon, Matthew MacFadyen as Demetrius, John Lloyd Fillingham as Lysander, Katy Brittain as Hermia, Rebecca Egan as Helena and Ian Hughes as Puck.

Opposite, bottom: With Amanda Harris as Titania.

Above, top: With Amanda, Ian and Christopher Benjamin as Bottom.

Above, bottom: With Amanda in the umbrella-bower.

Terry Smith / Getty Images

Alan Markfield

Top: "Why do we do it?" – with Dustin Hoffman in *The Merchant of Venice*.

Bottom: In my dressing room during the *Merchant*'s run.

TWELVE

I'm inspired by the magic of Mickey Feast at the matinee. I need a touch of it tonight: my throat is still swollen and throbbing.

I navigate my way along the uninspired concrete of the Barbican to the brothel. Before the evening performance I sit at my dressing room table staring into the mirror, my face encased in a Hannibal Lecter mask connected to a steam machine, I inhale the steam over my vocal chords for fifteen minutes. I then gargle, I sip Throat-Coat tea, I suck Vocalzone and Fisherman's Friend lozenges. On voice only when necessary, on whisper to my dresser and everyone else who drops by the brothel.

I'm told Christopher Benjamin has fallen over and hurt himself. I visit him in his dressing room next door. Chris has injured his knee, I whisper commiseration. Chris is listening to an old recording of Ernest Lough, a boy soprano, singing "O For the Wings of a Dove" on his cassette radio. Pure, sweet, touchingly innocent sound.

"What are you sucking?" Chris asks.

"A Fisherman's Friend, my voice is still a bit rough," I whisper.

He tries to cheer me with the story of an old gay actor who was arrested for importuning in a men's public lavatory. The actor is ordered to appear in court and whilst being questioned in the witness box develops a nervous cough.

"Would you like to suck on a Fisherman's Friend?" asks the sympathetic judge.

And the actor says,

"Oh, no thank you dear, I think I'm in enough trouble as it is."

I rasp a laugh.

But the rest of the evening is no joke.

Despite kind assurances from other cast members, I feel I just about manage to get through the show, but by the last scene my voice is weak and hurting. The cast's sympathetic smiles only serve in telling me I have a problem. I want the wings of a dove, I want to fly, to soar, but my vocal wings are clipped. I want to climb, hover and swoop like an eagle, but by the end of the play I have only a dying budgerigar twittering and choking to death in my throat. That's how it feels exactly. Small bird lodged in my swollen throat, dead or dying.

A triple piss-off day.

Piss-off number one. It's Twiggs' birthday. I'm in London doing a play. She's in America doing a film, back in Carolina after the hurricane, continuing the TV movie. First time we've been apart on either of our birthdays in all the years we've been together. I am very depressed and unhappy being apart from her on her birthday. These are occasions when we should be together. I have a second sense her film is going to go on through our wedding anniversary next week.

Piss-off number two. My voice is rough and I have two shows today.

Piss-off number three. I have had about six hours' sleep. I feel like shit. By 8 am I am in my second in a row of early morning cabs, to keep my new 9.30 am appointment in Rother-fucking-hithe with The Strangler.

By 10.15 am he has noted down my medical history and we have discussed his theory of treatment.

I lie on The Strangler's hard brown plastic-covered treatment table in the tiny room that serves as his surgery. The small 1970s-built terraced house is on a deeply depressing housing estate backing off a couple of industrial plants and builders' yard. The last place you'd expect a miracle, which is what I'm praying for.

A tall, black-haired, handsome man in his early forties, Jacob Liebermann, The Rotherhithe Strangler, sits on a stool behind my prostrate figure and works pulling and stretching my girder-stiff neck and manipulates my thumping, complaining head.

Liebermann is an Israeli, intelligent, intense and serious. I liked and trusted him immediately. He has the aura of a healer and he cares with a passion about his work. He doesn't smile much, but perhaps I think that only because my world is prone to smiling in a readily please-like-me theatrical capacity not called for in The Strangler's world of osteopathy.

He straightens out my body until my spine is flat on the table.

"How does that feel?" he asks.

"Feels good," I rasp.

With that he is at my throat like Nosferatu on the scent of blood, gripping and pulling my windpipe and voicebox. I'm amazed at just how malleable this tube of apparatus is – I mean how often do you have your windpipe grabbed like an inner tube pulled from its tyre, and survive? At least I hope I'll survive. I naturally stiffen and tense.

Nosferatu says, "No, no! you are tensing up. Try to stay relaxed."

After several attempts to stay relaxed until the moment I feel I will finally choke, he seems to think the morning's work complete.

"How does that feel?"

The answer I want to give will not awaken the dormant sense of humour in Nosferatu, so I repeat:

"Feels good."

But there is a God. A small miracle has occurred. In saying "Feels good" I notice a freedom, a relaxation in my throat.

"It will improve as the day goes on. I need to see you a few more times."

We make a future appointment.

"Goodbye," says my miracle-working vampire unsmilingly. But this boy is smiling.

At the matinee my voice is noticeably stronger, more flexible, by evening even stronger, despite the wear and tear of the matinee performance. I estimate it's an amazing 70 per cent better than last night. After a tentative careful start, I am able to risk some gentle vocal gymnastics. Still, as a precaution, I nurse and husband it through the two shows, thank God for Jacob Liebermann. But what of the morrow?

Before a lonely bedtime I whisper a "Happy Birthday" song to my wife via the satellites – it is her birthday here, but not yet her birthday in Carolina – very unsatisfying. We should be together. Worse news – filming is slow. It seems now she won't be back until even later, so it may be that she doesn't see the play at all in London and it has to be when we open in our next venue, Stratford upon Avon.

Getting a worrying number of injuries in the company now, inevitable when everyone is so exhausted. Bernard Lloyd, who plays Quince, has been off for a couple of days, pulled muscles in his legs due to the very steep rake on the stage. It does play hell with just about everyone's legs, knees and back. Let's hope Bernard is not the first of many to be off. His understudy, Hugh Parker, went on for him – he's much younger but made the part his own. Octavia Walters who plays First Fairy is having treatment for neck and back strain from clinging onto the umbrella she is suspended from in her first scene. Matthew Macfadyen, who plays Demetrius, has started getting badly bruised, not at all surprising the way he has to throw himself around; I'm constantly amazed he doesn't break his neck. John Lloyd Fillingham, who plays Lysander, is on antibiotics for an embarrassing and painful case of housemaid's knee as a result of all the kneeling his part requires on the unforgiving wooden-planked stage. Chris Benjamin is now also having vocal problems, and in addition has a Moses-type wooden staff added to his props to support his bulky figure to and from the stage as a result of his knee injury.

It's beginning to feel more like being a member of the Royal Infirmary than the Royal Shakespeare Company.

Amazingly, despite all this, the show continues to have an unquenchable joy, there's a spirit that transcends such earthly restrictions. The company is very solid and committed, I'm happy and lucky to be a part of it: one of the most talented and consistently committed collisions of actors one could wish to be spending time with, either side of the footlights. We are getting the most thrilling reception each and every performance – four, five or six cheering curtains tonight and most nights. I think we are all aware we are in something a bit special.

Up again at sparrow-fart this morning. This time to film excerpts from the play, on stage, to be used for TV advertising preceding and during the foreign leg of the tour.

Sadly, Steven O'Neil, who plays Flute brilliantly – the role that is, not the wind instrument – was unable to come in for filming because he injured his back in a fall at understudy rehearsal yesterday. Whoops, there goes another actor ker-plop.

My heart goes out to those in the company playing a part in the show and understudying another role at the same time. As well as doing the regular eight shows a week, they are called most mornings for understudy rehearsals.

Tony Blair, with his wife and two children came to see the show tonight. We were asked to stay in costume and congregate on the stage after the show to meet them. A slight feeling of resentment about this with some members of the company, they want to get out of sweaty costumes and wigs, take off make-up, have a pint at the pub, go home. We've just spent three hours sweating our bollocks off for you mate, why can't you come backstage like everyone else does? Other than the Royals of course. The leader of "New Labour" – which seems to be moving ominously ever closer to Old Tory – said he had "enjoyed the play", so had his wife and children. A formidable couple. There was something about them, though, an obvious affection. They are a team – we like that. Rumour has it he intends to introduce top-up fees for further education, a total betrayal of the Labour Party philosophy – we don't like that.

After a bit of self-conscious hanging around and hand-shaking, the huge pink padded umbrella that serves as Titania's bower is then lowered from the flies, down onto the stage, and the Blair kids were invited to a ride up and down in it. Standing around on stage in costume and make-up, watching the Blair kids going up and down like a Prime Minister's career, seemed a ludicrous waste of valuable time, so at this point I surreptitiously sidle off stage into the lift, up to my dressing room, change and slip out of the theatre to try and find a cab home. Taxis around the Barbican are as hard to find as a trusted politician, especially when the weather turns to rain, and all I want to do is get home and rest my still-troublesome vocal chords for the two shows tomorrow.

"Heigh Ho! The wind – and the rain."

Meantime, although the houses are very respectable in number, we are not sold out every weekday in London. I feel sure if more people knew we were on, we would be a full house all through the week. Our next venue in Stratford is almost sold out I hear. I'm assured the London posters arrive next week, and I'm told there was an ad in the *Independent* newspaper today for the play. We need more than word of mouth, and the inevitable GCSE school parties.

I'm ever so surprised at just how much I enjoy these school parties that come to see the show – they are fun to play to. I enjoy them more than I would have imagined I could. It gives a shiver of satisfaction to think that somewhere out there, enjoying the escape of the classroom for a matinee performance, or the treat of an evening in the theatre, may be experiencing *A Midsummer Night's Dream* or Shakespeare, or even the theatre itself for the very first time. For that someone – and it could quite possibly be just some *one* – their life will be changed forever. It's a heady responsibility.

"Hey, listen to this, you'll like it" – and some, some one young person, will leave our theatre and realise: "I liked that, think I'd like to be part of that one day". The seed is planted. That's it. There's no escape. You're the fortunate or unfortunate marked man or woman. It happened to me as a teenager going to Stratford upon Avon to see some of the early Peter Hall productions, still clear in my remembering. It makes me so incredibly happy to be part of that circle and perhaps infect a susceptible victim across the footlights.

The sales for the rest of the UK tour are very good indeed, some performances already sold out. Our company manager Neil Constable tells me he has a quest to top the last best box office figures an RSC tour, and it looks as if we might.

The Press Office sent me a resumé of our reviews so far. They are a conundrum of differing views. Comparisons are odious, but some seem compelled to say ours is better than the original production. Some seem to have come with preconceived prejudices as a result of that. It's weird and wonderful and makes no sense at all, that some critics should come and see the same play and say it's better than the original, and another chides it for being a revival. Are they aware in some European countries – in Russia for instance, since Stanislavski's day – a popular production can continue to be performed for years with different casts, as in the ballet or opera? My own, and I think the rest of the company's, faith and confidence in this production, is unwavering whatever I read. We are neither shaken nor stirred. If you believe the good reviews, you have to believe the bad ones. Best to stick to one's own opinion.

A visit to The Strangler. He's brilliant, just brilliant. Extremely painful for a second or two, but it's working. I continue to massage and manipulate my throat à la Liebermann throughout the day, every day. It helps and much more of a voice tonight. Very good show. Audience extremely receptive. Four or five curtains again. Bravos, standing ovation, clapping with their hands above their heads. Very encouraging and very appreciated by the company. This sort of reception has happily become the norm.

A short time after I'd been offered Oberon, an actor I know rang me when he'd heard I was playing the part. This guy is a good actor but notoriously lacking in the generosity department.

"I hear you've been offered Oberon at the RSC."

"Yeah, that's right."

"I played him a while ago. Shall I tell you about Oberon?"

"Yes please," I say desperate for insight or advice.

"Well the thing you should know about Oberon is he has to be on stage every performance for 20 minutes watching the lovers' quartet scene (*raucous laugh*), the longest scene in Act One (*raucous laugh*), after a couple of weeks it's the longest 20 minutes of your fucking life (*raucous laugh*). You're so bored you want to slash your fucking throat (*raucous laugh*)."

"Well thanks for sharing your secrets, mate. Is that it?"

A cackle from the other end of the phone tells me that's all I'm getting.

He was right. I do have to watch the longest scene in Act One every performance.

He was wrong. It isn't boring – not in our production, anyway. Especially not tonight.

It's a minefield out there.

I'm perched on top of the red downstage door that elevates me ten feet into the air where I sit and watch the lovers' scene in the wood. Puck is similarly perched observing from his yellow elevated door upstage.

The choreography and fight arrangements for the scene are complex and potentially dangerous. The physical energy and mental concentration of the quartet is tremendous. They and the audience have fun together and their work is always rewarded with much deserved spontaneous rounds of applause during and after the scene.

Tonight, from my elevated bird's-eye view, I'm alarmed to see large splats and trails of crimson colour appearing all over the stage. When John carries Katy over his shoulder I notice Katy's purple dress has large dark stains on it. The trails of crimson continue to appear zigzagging across and up and down the stage. Where the hell is it coming from?

I glance up to the flies high above the stage. Is some careless prat spilling paint up there? Unlikely, but at times like this anything seems possible. I'm beginning to get alarmed. The other actors individually become aware of the innovative new shade of red being indecorously introduced to our set. They are all barefoot and it is obviously wet and slippery. They carry on with the scene but I can see as each one notices the Hansel and Gretel trails leading nowhere in the wood, that they are increasingly bewildered and becoming concerned. *Where the hell is it coming from?*

John's white muslin trousers are now looking like a surgeon's after a busy day in the operating theatre. I hear some murmurs out front; one or two in the audience are beginning to notice.

I steal a glance upstage to Ian perched on his yellow door top. Ian's eagle eye misses nothing, I can see he's alarmed. I follow his gaze to John's right hand. His index finger is dripping with blood with the consistency of a tap that badly needs a new washer. Everyone on stage becomes transfixed with John's bleeding finger. Everyone, that is, except John, who seems blissfully unaware of his dribbling finger tap.

Five minds osmotically transmit one thought to John.

"Your finger, it's your finger. For fuck's sake look at your finger, John!"

John looks at his finger.

But what to do? White muslin trousers, green silk shirt, that's it. Nothing to wrap around the finger faucet.

Now I can see stage management and other members of the cast watching from the wings. Will they have to stop the show, dress his finger, mop the stage?

John tries to hide his hand behind his back or under his other arm. No good – it just draws more attention to it, and he has doors to open and close, people to catch and carry. He smiles, I think to let us on stage know he's not in pain. That strange phenomenon, Doctor Theatre, kicks in on such occasions.

But I can feel the audience becoming uncomfortable, concerned. I'm uncomfortable and concerned. Ian, Matthew, Rebecca and Katy are uncomfortable and concerned – the only one not uncomfortable and concerned appears to be the source of all the discomfiture and concern.

"Put your finger in your mouth, suck your finger!" I want to shout at him.

He puts his finger in his mouth.

But then again, speaking Shakespeare with your finger in your mouth is one exercise they forgot to teach us in the voice classes. John sucks his finger at regular intervals and they manage to get through the scene. Huge relief is felt by all as John exits to get his finger quickly attended to before his next entrance. It transpires he ripped his finger open on a piece of metal protruding from the doorframe. He's fine now, and did the rest of the play with his finger bandaged and wrapped like a huge white German bratwurst sausage. A source of much amusement, on stage and off, for the rest of the evening. John now has a housemaid's knee and a bratwurst sausage for a finger. I'm getting rather concerned there's going to be very little of the original actor left by the time we finish the tour.

*

"The remarkable thing about
Shakespeare is that he is really
very good – in spite of all the
people who say he is very good."
Robert Graves

On rare occasions, a play may call for eye-to-eye contact with a member or members of the audience. If, as in the majority of productions, this is not called for, I blur the audience, visually. I don't know how this happens. Obviously some self-induced myopic thing automatically takes place. On most occasions it serves me well and is very useful for concentration especially for a part like Oberon, where a good deal of it is delivered out front. I can see some of the audience, but they are very out of focus. Unless playing "in the round", after the first row or two of a proscenium theatre, the auditorium becomes gradually darker beyond the light spilling from the stage. So when looking out front, one sees only a sort of smoky black mirage punctuated by four or five green or red neon exit lights at the back and sides of the auditorium. This only, of course, if you are not already blinded by the glare of a spotlight.

This afternoon's matinee performance was packed. The audience intelligent, perceptive and receptive, and with us every inch of the way, every word. Particularly one gentleman sitting dead centre front row. How do I know if I can't see the audience? I know because some actors do look at the audience, see them clearly, and report anything unusual to another member of the cast, and it passes through the company faster than a poker-player can shuffle a pack.

The news can be passed between players on stage as well as off. For instance, in the Theseus and Hippolyta court scene for the play within the play, the stage is peopled with groups of courtiers who are required to mumble, murmur or whisper to each other with unscripted responses to the main action of the play. This sort of set-up provides a perfect, undetectable forum for the passing of covert information. The exchanges are by necessity usually brief and to-the-point.

This afternoon, about half an hour before the end of the play, when we were a little way through the scene where Bottom and his mates perform their wedding nuptial play for Theseus, Hippolyta and their court, Amanda as Hippolyta turned upstage, gave me a sweet loving honeymoon smile, and whispered romantically in my ear, "Front row centre".

In a moment I had a chance to steal a focused look at the man sitting front row centre. I wish I hadn't. No, not a dirty perv playing with himself. Or some old biddy clicking away with her knitting needles. Not a famous person looking bored. Not someone asleep, not someone dead. All the above have been known.

No, this was in some way worse and quite new to me. The man sitting front row centre was a large, bespectacled, tweed-jacketed, grey-bearded, donnish-looking specimen, glaring alternately from the stage to the thick open book he was holding in his outstretched hands. As he did so, he moved his reading glasses up to rest on his forehead to look at the stage, then down again to the bridge of his nose to read from the book, up to his forehead to look at the stage, down to his nose to read the book, ad infinitum. If I'd been the unfortunate person sitting either side of him I'd have been subjected to a huge desire to ram the tome up his jacksey.

I look at Hippolyta with the adoring longing of a new husband, whisper in her ear,

"What the fuck's he doing?"

She laughs in character, strokes my cheek lovingly and smilingly whispers,

"Complete Works, checking lines."

The "Complete Works" is the *Complete Works of Shakespeare*. The don is sitting front row centre checking us line by line with his Complete Works! He couldn't get a slim copy of only *A Midsummer Night's Dream*? He has to sit on the front row with a huge white tome? Moving his glasses up and down like a piston? He's checking our lines?

Yes, of course we are word-perfect, but this is not the time to remind us of that. The whole problem you see, you tweeded twat, is going through the agony of learning lines and then forgetting they are someone else's and making them your own. It's a very tricky business, you bearded piston prat. It's very hard to do, and you are seriously hindering the process. At this point the last thing an actor wants to be reminded of is that the lines he is speaking were written by somebody else and are being policed by a self-appointed Shakespeare traffic warden. We have a prompter in the wings should we require one. If you really need your book, sit at the back with a pen torch.

The learning process and performance are two separate entities. Even when appearing in a play by a living author it's impossible to imagine he would sit on the front row in performance, checking the cast have learned his lines. This one's been dead 400 years. Who is this self-appointed emissary from the celestial library?

I still have a couple of long monologues to deliver before the end of the play.

Will he tut-tut if I go wrong? Or shout out a line if I pause longer than he deems necessary?

My automatic blur switch malfunctions. The rest of the audience disappear alright, but now, all I seem to be able to see, wherever I look, is the obsessed don sitting front row centre, piston-turning pages, checking me on my lines. It's an unbelievably thoughtless, insensitive distraction. I'm unnerved and annoyed, but some of the company are even more perturbed – and furious.

At the curtain calls, I find myself standing directly above the insensitive Blimp, he's only two feet away. As the applause continues from all in the audience except Blimp, I manage to catch his eye, give him a beaming smile, and whisper,

"Was I all right on my lines, you prat?"

He nods a quick nod which I choose to interpret as an affirmative and diverts his eyes back to the tome resting on his lap.

There's nowt as queer as folk.

THIRTEEN

Sunday today, what bliss! A free clear day, just me, Theseus and Oberon, rattling around the kitchen or quietly padding from room to room. Alone, but not lonely. I'm happy with the company I keep.

Speak to Twiggs. The happy news is, looks like she can make it home for next Friday and see our last performance in London the following day. She has only two days more filming to do in Carolina, then two days in New York to do some press interviews and TV chat shows promoting her new album *London Pride*, then home. The album is receiving some wonderful reviews in the music press in America. There are four or five tracks that I think are blindingly good. I sometimes forget just what a talented girl my girl is.

Linda McCartney rings to see how the show is going and discusses a time when they can come and see it. She says she's going to America to try a new treatment. Oh God, I hope it works. Said she thinks about us a lot, misses us, and is sorry we can't meet up more because of our various work commitments at the moment. To write in our diaries in big letters that we are to go down to Kent with Carly and Ace to stay with them for a time during the month I have off over Christmas. She's an angel, funny and brave. I love this woman. She's a wonderful wife to Paul and mother to their kids, and friend to us. We need people like her on the planet.

Spent a few hours locked away with Oberon and Theseus working on the passages we're not yet totally happy or comfortable with. We got a few glimpses worth pursuing.

Last night, waiting in the wings to go on for my first Oberon scene. I sit backstage and look around to see costumed members of the cast lying on the huge velvet cushions used in Act Two, whispering, laughing, holding hands, hugging, listening – the whole sight reminiscent of a 1960s "love-in".

My own journey is to destroy the demons preventing me from fully enjoying every moment and aspect of the two parts I am playing. At times I find myself wishing to play only Oberon without the burden of Theseus' huge and somewhat less rewarding role. I long for the luxury of coming on stage as Oberon, playing the wonderfully woven scenes and getting off. It's a cherry-on-the-cake part.

Changing into Theseus on stage by the mere switching of cloaks still concerns me. I've heard some of the audience are confused by this too. There is inevitably a compromise made in playing the two roles. It's still an exacting challenge.

It's now about six weeks since we started rehearsals. Again, it feels as if I've never done anything else in my life but this play. As if my previous life was a dream and now I find myself curiously once more in a dream on stage, and off.

*

"Too caustic? To hell with cost,
we'll make the picture anyway."
Samuel Goldwyn

One of the greatest sources of amusement to the gods must be when they look down and observe mortals making plans for the future. I expect they had a quiet chuckle today when my wife rang me with the news from Carolina.

"Hello." Her voice is a flat monotone.

My hear sinks.

I recognise this tone.

I know from her voice she's got "Hello" the wrong way round – this is really an "Ohell" call. She's obviously very upset.

It means there's a problem

"What's the matter?" I say.

"There's a problem."

The shorthand of repetition in a relationship is a great time-saver.

"Surprise me!"

And she does.

Yesterday four men dressed in long black overcoats, black trilby hats and dark glasses, looking like they'd stepped out of a 1930s gangster movie, flew into Carolina, turned up unannounced on the film set, and closed the film down.

"Un-fucking-believable," I say, "who are they?"

"We don't know."

Carolina is a non-union state, but a lot of the film crew are union members. As I understand the story so far, the crew were told by Bugsy, Scarface, Knuckles, and Big Jake that if they continue on the film they would be blacklisted.

The working days have been long and gruelling to try and catch up on time lost due to the hurricane. It seems some member of the crew has been in touch with the Teamsters and the *Godfather* lookalikes were called in to sort it.

The secret plan now is to ostensibly close the film down, fly the cast to Los Angeles to give the impression its over, then secretly fly the cast, under false names, to Utah, another non-union State, and complete the remaining two days shooting with a crew already working in Utah on another movie.

I'm reminded now how the scenes behind the camera on a film production are so often more intriguing than the ones being shot.

But the bottom line is, we'll be apart for another week and Twiggs will miss the last night of the play in London and there will be an empty chair still at the dinner table this weekend.

It breaks my heart to hear her crying on the other end of the long-distance telephone line. She wants desperately to come home. But there's nought to be done.

I manage to reassure and talk her down a bit before the hated click, and she's gone, and we're in two separate hemispheres again.

Back in the safe-ish, less political world of the theatre, tonight's show was a blast. The reception at the end so overwhelming and emotive, dear old John Warner, who is coming up to his 76th birthday, was moved to tears at the curtain call, and still bleary-eyed on his way back to the dressing rooms.

Emotions running high on both sides of my world. Four more days in London. Then a week off. Then Stratford upon Avon.

Although wifeless, the last night in London was overwhelmingly, blisteringly sparking and glitteringly memorable.

The whole show took off again and flew. It had a life, a world of its own. When I stepped on stage I was enfolded into the world of the play. When I stepped out of the light into the wings that world disappeared.

I was time-travelling. I'd like more of that please.

My girl is back. Arrived home yesterday. Sadly for us both, she missed the last night in London. No matter, we open in Stratford end of the week. In some ways better there than in London.

So there you are, you see. All's well that ends. We finished the London run of the play. Twiggs is home.

Oh, and we have two new kittens.

*

"Lat take a cat, and foster him wel
With milk
And tender flesh, and make him couche
Of silk,
And lat him see a mouse go by the
Wal,
Anon he wyveth milk, and flesh, and
Al,
And every deyntee which is in that
hous,
Swich appetyt hath he to ete a mouse."

Chaucer

At the airport she appears around the Customs barrier, tanned, blonde, beautiful. I'm a sort of green and a wreck. That strange shyness on meeting and kissing again, for a flicker like a first date. On the way out of the airport I say,

"We have to make a brief detour to choose something."

"What is it?" she asks excitedly.

"Wait and see," I excitedly reply.

I'm a bit nervous as we ascend the stairs to the feral cat flat. Is this a bad idea after all? Worries unfounded. A gasp of delight as the living room door is opened and she spies the black and white bundles. The biggest of the litter wobbles over to her. She sits on the floor as he approaches.

"This one," she says.

"How do you know?" I say astonished at the speed of choice.

"I just know."

The "chosen one" spends all his time with his sister, a little black bundle with green eyes. The choice is made easy.

A week and two visits later we adopt them both.

But what to do when we go to Stratford? I'm told no pets allowed in the RSC apartments that we'll be staying in.

Farewell London. I'm going home.

Stratford upon Avon

FOURTEEN

"Hear hills do lift their heads
Aloft from whence sweet
Springs doe flow
Whose moistur good doth
Furtil make the valieis
Couchte belowe.
Hear goodly orchards
Planted are in fruite
Which doe abounde
Thine ey wolde make their
Hart rejoice to see
So pleasant grounde"
*On 16th century tapestry map of
the shire of Warwickshire woven
by Richard Hyckes*

I'm home. I'm in Warwickshire. My father's family is entirely Glaswegian Scottish. My mother's family London East End. They were evacuated here during World War Two.

I was born here. I grew up here.

When I think of Warwickshire, I think of trees, I think of green, I think of history, I think of my boyhood, I think of Shakespeare. It's a magical county full of ghosts, national and personal.

Stratford upon Avon has its own magic. No doubt about that. The old man's ubiquitous presence envelops the old parts of town still. Trinity Church, the Grammar School, the cobbled, dimly-lit lanes, the 15th-century bridge and the timeless river running beneath it, belong to Him entirely now. His presence is palpable everywhere. It isn't a new discovery for me. I grew up a short distance away.

As a schoolboy bunking school I would pedal my truant bike through the country lanes in rhythm and harmony with the buzzing hedgerows, to Kenilworth, Warwick and Stratford upon Avon, the risky adventure amply rewarded by all I saw around me. No contest between the danger involved and the rewards received in undertaking the truant adventures.

There are reams of surmised theories written about Shakespeare. Countless scholars and academics – centuries and cemeteries full of writers – have, with a seemingly uncontrollable didactic compulsion, proposed and tried to substantiate all sorts of theories, forcing and conjuring the flimsiest of sources, historical and literal collaborations to support a view, to sustain a theory. At the end of the day, a lot of it can be taken as nothing more than supposition. When I was rehearsing *Yonadab*, a new play by Peter Shaffer, at the National Theatre some years ago, I shared a taxi home with the author and he told me he was constantly amazed when being interviewed or reading about his work, what some people had decided he meant by a particular play or piece. He said what he does, is try to write a good play and tell an interesting story, and how ridiculous it appeared to him to see aspects of his work analysed and intellectualised beyond his own recognition.

But some folk seem unable to resist the temptation. It's sometimes interesting, or perhaps reassuring, to involve these academic theories in the research of a play, but in the end they can be no more than that – a theory, an hypothesis. Maybe interesting to know but for the actor in the final analysis it's head *and* heart that makes for a true performance. Shakespeare's plays were written to be acted, not dissected to death in the schoolroom and lecture hall.

About two dozen well-authenticated facts are known about Shakespeare's actual life, but libraries of books have been written by all sorts of different people, putting forward all sorts of different theories to fill in the gaps in the hope of proving, or disproving, the Stratford Poet's phenomenal genius.

Here's the story as it came to me. The facts:

William Shakespeare's father, John Shakespeare, was a prosperous businessman and person of importance in the municipal affairs of Stratford, already by then a thriving market town. John held for a year the office of Bailiff, and afterwards became Chief Alderman. He married Mary Arden, or Mary Hard-On as she was known to us when, as a schoolboy, I would cycle there with a friend while playing truant from school, finding it no hard task at all to conjure up these vivid ghosts in the largely unchanged settings. John Shakespeare married Mary Hard-On, the daughter of a wealthy farmer from the neighbouring village of Wilmcote. With her came land and houses.

William, their third and eldest surviving child, was born in Stratford upon Avon in 1564. His date of birth is not known but his date of baptism is. Recorded at Trinity Church, Stratford, 26th April, 1564 as Gulielmus Johannes Shakspere.

A few years later, however, John fell into debt and was forced to mortgage his wife's property. Of John and Mary's surviving children, three boys and two girls younger than William, only the boys were entitled to a free education at the grammar school that still exists in Stratford.

In the small village of Shottery, a short distance from Stratford, there's a cottage known still as Anne Hathaway's Cottage or "Anne Have-It-Away's Cottage", as she was known to us truants, aware as we were that our local hero lad, "Will", had got her pregnant and had to marry her. This story seemed to make them very real and accessible to us for some reason.

> "Anne Hathaway, she hath a way
> To charm all hearts Anne Hathaway..."

would be recited by me and my skiving mate as we sat in her garden eating the sandwiches our mothers had made for school lunch, washed down with a shared bottle of dandelion and burdock bought with our school tuck money from the cornershop in Shottery. The garden was to me the most beautiful I had ever seen, stocked as it was, and still is, with borders bursting with a breath-taking kaleidoscope of colours. Flowers and herbs, heady scents, butterflies and bees.

> "I know a bank where the wild thyme blows,
> Where oxlips and the nodding violet grows;
> Quite o'ercanopied with luscious woodbine,
> With sweet musk roses and with eglantine;
> There sleeps Titania some time of the night,
> Lull'd in these flowers with dances and delight;
> And there the snake throws her enamell'd skin,
> Weed wide enough to wrap a fairy in:"

When Anne's father, Richard Hathaway, died, he left his daughter about £7 for her wedding portion; and the cottage and farm to his widow and son.

It's generally accepted that Anne Have-It-Away was Shakespeare's wife but late in 1582, the day before the bishop gave authorisation for the marriage to take place, his registrar recorded the bride as "Anne Whateley of Temple Grafton", another tantalising temptation for scholarly speculation. William is listed in the register as William Shagspear, aptly named we boys thought under the circumstances and worth a giggle, and here's the reason why. When Will Shagspear married Anne Have-it-Away he was eighteen years old. She was twenty-six and three months pregnant. How do we know? Because the Register of Holy Trinity Church, Stratford upon Avon, records the Baptism of Susanna, Daughter of William Shakespeare, in May 1583, about six months after the marriage. A year and a half later, it records the christening of twins: a son, Hamnet, and daughter, Judith, to the Shakespeare couple.

It would appear the next seven-year period of Shakespeare's life, of which absolutely nothing is known – and I mean nothing – offers would-be biographers the greatest opportunity to sell books and talk twaddle. Pages of tropes. Mountains of metaphorical misinformation and fanciful speculation on his life, as a butcher, a poacher, schoolteacher, a soldier, a sailor, a lawyer, a wandering player, or travelling to northern Italy, or setting up business in London as a horse-minder.

The only slightly tenuous connection with fact in any of the above is that the final suggestion would have offered an opportunity for young Will to observe some of the horse-shit that was later to be written about him.

His name next appears, or is alluded to, in 1592, in London, in a written attack by another writer, Robert Greene, which indicates that Shakespeare was by then acting and writing. A year later a fellow Stratfordian, Richard Field, a printer, also at that time living in London, published Shakespeare's poem, *Venus and Adonis*, his first appearance in print.

Now, there are many other bits and bobs of interesting information known about his immediate family and they offer a tantalising glimpse of life then, but very small insight into the man himself.

There are some publishing dates of his 38 plays and 154 sonnets in Folio or Quarto form, although the dating of his plays can sometimes appear to be more confident and accurate than perhaps they should. To my knowledge, about a dozen or so facts remain concerning the man himself. He's mentioned, amongst other players, who received money for plays presented before Queen Elizabeth I. In 1596 his son Hamnet died, aged eleven years. In the same year, Shakespeare was granted a coat of arms in Stratford upon Avon and a writ was issued which bound him to keep the peace, but we don't know what prompted this. Twelve months later, he bought "New Place", the second largest house in Stratford, some cottages and a barn, and is reported for non-payment of tax by the Tax Collector of Bishopsgate in London. He is named as a shareholder in the land for the Globe Theatre on the South Bank, and again recorded as owing taxes, as he is again a year later for non-payment in Sussex.

In 1601 John Shakespeare, his father, died and the following year William bought over a hundred acres of farmland

and a cottage in Stratford. The last record of him acting in public theatre was in 1603. In 1604 he is mentioned as appearing at the coronation of King James I, by now a wealthy and successful man and a member of "The King's Men" theatre company. Women were not allowed to appear on stage at this time, of course. Many of his plays appear in court performance records. In 1607 his daughter, Susanna, married John Hall, an eminent and much respected doctor in Stratford. His house and herb garden still exist next to the site of Shakespeare's house, "New Place", now demolished. A year later his granddaughter, Elizabeth, is born and his mother, Mary Hard-on Shakespeare, dies. In 1613 William buys more property, this time in London – the Blackfriars Gatehouse, not far from the Globe Theatre which was destroyed by fire in the same year. There was later yet another lawsuit concerning the Blackfriars property.

It is mainly as a result of the various legal proceedings that six of Shakespeare's signatures survive, although the spellings vary a good deal. Three of these signatures on his will which is signed on March 25, 1616, remembering his friends but leaving the bulk of his estate to his daughter, Susanna. He died exactly a month later, recorded in Trinity Church, Stratford upon Avon, April 25, 1616: "Will Shakespeare, Gent".

Famously, the only thing bequeathed in his will to his wife Anne Have-It-Away was his second-best bed.

That's about it really. Very little else is known about the man himself. I should check a few dates – although I find dates arse-achingly boring. It actually doesn't matter what he smoked in his pipe – what matters is the English language bred and then inherited a standard of writing that constantly astonishes and is still aspired to and envied by every writer on the planet four hundred years after his death. Shakespeare's work, unlike the dates surrounding it, isn't cold and boring, is not barren, not an alienating impenetrable mystery as he can become in the classroom; but warm and human, vital, wise and funny, layers of shimmering depths as enjoyable and accessible to an audience today as they were when he wrote them.

Something to be said then in defence of truanting and the happenstance of being almost in situ to soak up his all-embracing presence and the local stories that made it all so vivid to my boyish mind. History that was all around me. Villages almost unchanged in centuries. Kenilworth Castle, destroyed by Cromwell. Warwick Castle still miraculously intact and perfect.

But strangely it was the ruins of Kenilworth Castle that touched me most and held a vivid magic for me. As the afternoon sun cast shadows of times past over its broken walls, I would stand on the step of my favourite stone pillar in the ruins of the Great Hall, and without touching a button obtain instant play-back on my not-yet-invented virtual-reality headset.

All this to be had a short truant ride away: uncluttered with motor vehicles, the lanes would ring with only our piping prepubescent voices and bicycle bells. We knew – as Shakespeare would have as he walked these lanes, fields and meadows – what berries were good to eat, what plants and leaves to chew on should a snack be required, what freshwater springs we could scoop up in our cupped hands to drink from. All this and the information gleaned from local stories served to offer gloriously happy escape.

Would I have learned and been as excited by all this in the classroom? Possibly.

Would it be so cobwebbed in? Such a personal experience with our local literary hero? Probably not.

That feeling of awe felt as a boy standing in the chancel of Trinity Church, looking down for the first time on that simple slab gravestone and reading, until it was known by heart:

> "Good friend for iesus sake forbeare,
>   To digg the dvst enclosed heare.

Blese be Ye man Yt spares thes stones:
And cvrst be he Yt moues my bones"

has never left me. The rest is silence.

FIFTEEN

"Thrice happy river, on whose fertile banks
The laughing daisies, and their sister tribes,
Violets, and cuckoo buds, and lady-smocks,
With conscious pride, a brighter dye disclose,
And tell us Shakespeare's hand their charms
improved."

From "Edgehill" by Richard Iago 1767

A large slice of an actor's life is spent in hotel rooms and rented accommodations. The RSC has some apartments at Stratford that they rent out to the actors performing there. Avonside is the name of the small apartment block I'm staying in. As the name would suggest, it stands overlooking the River Avon. It's an unremarkable, three-storey, brick-built, 1980s job, located a ten-minute walk from the theatre and is saved by its location nestling, as it does, on the banks of the river a few hundred easy yards or so from the shadow of Trinity Church where Himself was christened and buried.

My "apartment" on the second floor consists of a basic but adequate kitchen, a short corridor, one bedroom with double bed and a living room with a small balcony that overlooks a bend in the river, and weir where flocks of river birds meet for a gossip: a bevy of swans, a paddling of ducks, a gaggle of geese, gather in a cacophony of sound. It's a beautiful romantic view that changes in the autumn light as the days draw into night, and the mornings drift into day.

Called for technical rehearsals at 10.30 am.

I walk from my apartment at Avonside, along the gravel path, a few yards more and I'm in the churchyard, say good-morning to Will resting inside Trinity Church and ask his help with the task ahead. It's a circle completed. A new unfathomable sense of continuity creeps into my soul and settles comfortably there. It's an impossible task to analyse a soul. I'm home.

I continue along the grassy banks of the River Avon escorted by tourist-tolerant ducks and swans loudly and unembarrassedly chiding the empty-handed actor for not thinking to bring his breakfast leftovers.

The huge edifice of the Stratford Memorial Theatre as if floating on the brown water breaks and blocks the view. Described by some as ugly, to me it signals the beauty of the Taj Mahal. Almost a sacred place. A temple certainly.

I sign my name in the stage door book, and am given the key to dressing room number 1A. Ghosts, ghosts all around. My dressing room windows has doors that open onto an even smaller balcony overlooking the Green Room terrace and beyond to the gently flowing reaches of the Avon, straddled by Hugh Clopton's fifteenth-century stone bridge still used as the main thoroughfare into Stratford.

Hugh Clopton was a native of Stratford who not only built bridges, but also became Lord Mayor of London and set a precedent for Shakespeare and other Warwickshire lads to "go south young man".

No make-up required, but change into costume for the first technical rehearsal. Stepping onto the hallowed boards of the main stage for the first time is an intoxicating euphoric cocktail of fear and commitment renewed. One cannot escape the footprints of performances past. Are they somehow present still? Underneath the stage? In the wings? Above us in the flies? Listening? Looking? Commenting?

The technical rehearsal is slow and fraught with problems. The gi-normous block of computerised machinery and mile of cable installed to control the dozens of descending lights, the rising doors, and body-bags that elevate Puck, me and the young lovers twelve feet above the stage, seems confused by its own technology, or someone does; it's so advanced it doesn't work.

It's a long hard day and by the time we break it's dark outside. Stratford is closed. I clip-clop my way along the cobbled street in a homeward direction. Pass the famous Dirty Duck pub, lights and noises from within, but doors firmly closed.

"Come and have a drink," says a voice behind me.

It's Amanda Harris and a couple of others from the company.

"Looks closed."

"They'll open for us," she says with confidence and a smile that lights up the dim street.

Inside, gaggles of actors and techies sit around the small room in noisy groups. The walls are lined with dozens of framed black and white photographs of company actors past, looking down, frustrated not to be participating tonight in the bawdy or intimate cliques that make up the present company in the cosy room.

This bar room doesn't appear to have changed since, as a youth, I would self-consciously stand, pint in hand, at the bar, overawed and intimidated at the close proximity of the actors I'd just seen across the road on stage. Longing with an aching heart to be part of that fraternity. But how to do it? How? Where do you start?

Pam Harris runs the Dirty Duck pub and has as long as anyone can remember, well, as long as I can remember. A friendly, middle-aged, blonde widow, she is warm and welcoming with a firm no-nonsense side, that usefully comes into play when at closing time the general public are asked to finish their drinks, and leave, and favoured members of the Company encouraged to have another drink, and stay. A "Members Only" atmosphere kicks in the moment the last complaining civilian is ushered out through Pam's pub doors.

"I used to come in here 30 years ago before I was an actor," I tell Pam.

"Yes, I remember you," she says.

"What? No, you can't, you're thinking of someone else."

"No, I'm not – I remember you." No-nonsense side terminating any further possibility of doubt.

"And before we go any further down Memory Lane, I want to ask for your photo for the wall."

"Honoured and privileged, Pam."

And I am.

To be included in the Dirty Duck Hall of Fame feels like winning the Olivier Award for Most Promising Newcomer.

We settle around a table with lagers and packets of crisps, and the chat quickly turns to the Company obsession, Shakespeare and all things theatrical.

Have I died and gone to heaven?

I walk home alone. The mellow yellow street lights reflected onto the wet, ancient, stone-slabbed pavement like splashes of gold paint. The river, black as a bible, burbles on, ever on, to my left towards Trinity Church. On my right, the Rembrandt light from the cottage windows spills into their pretty gardens. A few dozen steps and I'm into the deathly quiet churchyard. Not a branch whispers. Not a leaf murmurs. Still. Quiet as a church mouse. Quiet as the grave.

No, not frightening at all. What's the opposite of frightened? I don't know. Comfortable? That'll do. I feel comfortable.

The autumn leaves have hardly yet begun to fall from the tall limes that stand sentry along the edge of the narrow gravestone-lined track. Only a few parched old-timers from the oak are blown aside like yesterday's confetti, leading me to the church.

I pause by the great old oak door of the chancel. Locked and bolted firm.

He's in there. He's lying in there.

My finger traces down the grey weathered door. I push a fingernail against a lesion, its surface hard as iron.

He's in there. He's lying in there. On the other side of the fossiled door all the secrets lie. Help me, help me to reach this part, these parts. Somehow transfer to me a guidance that could make you feel proud of what this Warwickshire lad is trying to do. I want your approval.

Speciali Gratia – sanction, assent, acquiescence, dispensation.

Almost, almost I can hear a whisper.

"Just do the best you can and let me keep my secrets."

An owl hoots, a crow craws, the bruised clouds claim the moon. On such a night as this he wrote:

> PUCK: "For night's swift dragons cut the clouds full fast,
> And yonder shines Aurora's harbinger,
> At whose approach ghosts wandering here and there
> Troop home to churchyards. Damned spirits all,
> That in the cross-ways and floods have burial,
> Already to their wormy beds are gone,
> For fear lest day should look their shames upon;
> They wilfully themselves exile from light,
> And must for aye consort with black-brow'd night."

Crunch along the pebblestone path that leads to Avonside. My life seems to have settled into a feeling of rightness. Here, at Avonside, my Havenside.

> "I never knew one moment's peace like this.
> Here, in this little soft retreat...
> My life glides on, and all is well within."

My secret co-habitees, the kittens, are with me.

There's a domesticity about being here that appeals to me. A feeling almost of being a student again. It gives a certain rooting and grounding that I need after the vagaries of a night in the theatre. Safe, cosseted and secure, contained within my own world. Not complacent I hope, but certainly content. Am I getting old? Or just wise? Bit of both I suppose. It would be churlish to deny that old friend fate is looking kindly down on the Warwickshire lad with the reward of near-perfect, almost aloneness.

In the small room, only the burbling rush of the weir beyond my window. Sweet solitude. Force myself to go to bed before the approach of Aurora's harbinger, the dawn ducks, and the good morning geese, announce the start of a new Stratford day and the end of an actor's night.

SIXTEEN

Oberon and Theseus still at times feel like old steam locomotives – surprisingly, Oberon in particular – I have to work and drive him along, continually, stoke the engine, watch the dials, negotiate the signals. Slow down for a turn, speed up on the straights. Nothing seems to be on automatic yet, God knows if it ever will be.

I find myself straining at my throat again at times – it's driving me crazy – the result of being too much angst-ridden me, and not enough over-confident Theseus and Oberon, possibly.

After a matinee and evening performance, I own I'm sometimes sick of the sound of my own voice and wish Theseus would just shut-the-fuck-up. I long for my characters to play me all the way through the play, not me to play them. Trying not to push for this, staying relaxed enough to let this happen, until the magic kicks in, is a conundrum. It comes and goes.

Perfection never can be attained in acting, of course, it's an impure art, I know that, but no point in settling for less. It's a non-negotiable quest.

My fear of being unsympathetic and too heavy in the first Oberon scene was unfounded. My worry was that when I did want to introduce an element of fun and mischief, I'd already gone too far down the road of darkness for the audience to be able to accept the other, funnier, mischievous elements of his character later in the play. With this release I find I'm able to build in some humorous moments, which I, and they, seem to enjoy very much indeed.

Today, at the Theatre, standing on the Green Room smoker's terrace overlooking the river, I fell into chatting about this with David Troughton, who I am told is superb as Lopakhin in *The Cherry Orchard* at present playing in the Swan Theatre. It rang a familiar bell to hear him say that after nine months of playing the role, he now wanted to recall everyone who had ever seen it and say:

"Look, come and see it now, I've got it right now – or righter."

The theatre is knackering all right. I sleep an inordinate amount, nine to ten hours a night now, and rest between shows on matinee days. I pace myself carefully, everything geared to the performance. It's a different form of fatigue to doing a film or TV series. Not a 5 am, but a 7 pm call. No two-minute takes. When you're on, you're on. For two and a half hours.

On the other hand, I feel a rejuvenation by working in the theatre, having spent a good half of my professional life in film and TV. I have for the most part enjoyed that, but I don't need it, I need the theatre. I couldn't live without it. That's why I became an actor.

Also it's nice to have a lie-in in the morning.

*

"When the heart is afire, some
sparks will fly out of the mouth"
Thomas Fuller (1654–1734)

I've just returned from a sensational evening in the Temple of Excellence. Again our audience tonight were marifical. The cast were on heat. Us or them? Both. It's a two-way trade-off.

Tonight's audience just blew us away with their intense enthusiasm. There is no experience you can liken to the mutual magic that takes place in the theatre on such a night as this. They seemed to understand everything we were trying to do; we were partners, and as a result we made some leaps forward together.

For my part I suspect I made a few breakthroughs tonight. Oberon and Theseus clearer and simpler. Vocally trying not to push it. Thanks to the Strangler, I'd estimate my voice is about 95 per cent back to normal. Taking my time where I need to, and getting on with it where necessary. Being bold. Not falling into old, safe patterns.

So easy to fall into these old patterns, habits and inflexions – sometimes quite scary to dare to change them, or hear them change themselves. Then to find something almost beyond your control is taking over and a monologue, speech, line, or a word emerges from your mouth in a way that surprises even the messenger.

Words are the end product of thoughts. New thoughts spawn new sounds. End result? New, living, poetry.

The Theseus and Hippolyta opening scene seems to be almost taking care of itself now. The pace has smartened up; as characters we have a history and viability.

Shakespeare works better at a speedy pace; on the whole, you have to earn your pauses. If it's delivered too slowly and ponderously it can be dull and arse-achingly boring.

Oberon had a brio tonight. He didn't alienate the audience with his zealous, manipulative darker side, but it seemed to emphasise and contrast with his humour in a way that is becoming a delight to play.

I just can't wait to get on there and do it. But it's a delicate balance. Simplifying is often the key.

Tonight as Oberon squeezes the magic juice into Demetrius' eyes and casts the spell:

> "Flower of this purple dye,
> Hit with Cupid's archery,
> Sink in apple of his eye.
> When his love he does espy,
> Let her shine as gloriously
> As the Venus of the sky.
> When thou wak'st, if she be by,
> Beg of her for remedy."

Tonight, Oberon spoke the lines as if panicked by the messy situation Puck has got him into, and as a result can't think of a rhyming spell so "bends" the lines to rhyme.

> "... When his love he doth espy,
>   Let her shine as glorious–lye
>   As the Venus of the sky.
>   When thou wak'st, if she be by,
>   Beg of her for rem–er–dye."

A bit cheeky, I thought, but Oberon got himself a round of applause on this tonight. I was pleased for him.

This cast is quite extraordinary. Watching them every performance, their dedication to their work, their total professionalism is a yardstick for any company.

Had every intention of going for a drink with the company to the Dirty Duck after tonight's perf. But my feet walked on past the stone steps that lead to its door, preferring the hysterical kitten company of two secret companions and the contrasting quiet of my Haven more.

Mop Day or Fair Day in Stratford. A once-yearly fair called Mop Day has been in existence by Royal Charter in Stratford for centuries.

No one seems to know why it's called Mop Day. One theory is that unemployed labourers from neighbouring villages would come to Stratford in search of employment and distinguish their job-seeker status by wearing a mop hat.

The only people today making money from their labours were the fair rides and stalls, £1.50 and even £2.50 a go, or for a three-minute ride or three throws at a coconut. I wonder how the kids afford an afternoon at the fair these days?

Not a mop hat in sight by the way.

Had a great aromatherapy massage from Katy Slokum who also works as a dresser at the theatre, and arranged for her to do my neck and shoulders every night before the show. The tension in my shoulders and neck has built up over the last few weeks and sometimes it feels as if Godzilla's mighty hand has grabbed me by the back of the neck and won't let go.

Show went well despite the inevitability of dragging the hollow echo of last night's unmatchable experience with us.

Wishing, hoping, willing them to be the same but that sort of experience doesn't, can't, happen every night. As a result, didn't quite hook them all the way. Our fault. It seemed a bit of a slog throughout the evening, but then a tumultuous reception, shouts and whistles, people standing again, hands above their heads at the curtain.

*

> "I pass like night from land to land:
> I have strange power of speech."
> *Samuel Taylor Coleridge*

O happy day. Blessèd day. My voice has come back one hundred per cent. By that I mean the instrument has miraculously repaired and tuned itself fully overnight.

I don't know who visited. Or how it happened. I'm just ever so grateful it did.

I've been working on about 95 per cent but "bell tones" from head and face have remained at best unreliable, at worst elusive. This, despite the daily regime of a physical and vocal warm-up before each show. I massage my vocal chords, I have a neck and shoulder massage daily, I rest my voice when not on stage, I go home and sit silent after the play. And I pray.

Today I woke to find the honky-tonk Joanna had gone and been replaced with a Steinway Grand. So thrilled was I with my new instrument, I spent most of the second half of the play running up and down the keyboard like a kid unable to believe his punishment was over and his favourite toy has been returned to him.

Normally in *A Midsummer Night's Dream* the change from Bottom to the ass is achieved by using a false head. In our production the transformation is achieved by Christopher Benjamin, playing Bottom, exiting the stage and reappearing with donkey ears protruding through his 1950s crash helmet, a long tail attached to his baggy cord pants, and a large pair of yellowing donkey dentures fitted over his own teeth. This works extremely well. You can still see the actor through the disguise in a Jekyll and Hyde sort of way.

But the donkey dentures make speech rather difficult at times – too good an opportunity for the theatre gremlins to miss.

Tonight I was standing downstage right, leaning against the proscenium arch facing upstage to observe Bottom as the ass with Titania and her fairies lying in and around her bower. Bottom is reclining in the bower next to Titania, all very cosy and more than a little salacious.

Titania has just said:

> "Come sit thee down upon this flowery bed,
>   While I thy amiable cheeks do coy,
>   And stick musk-roses in thy sleek smooth head,
>   And kiss thy fair large ears, my gentle joy."

And Bottom replies:

> "Where's Peaseblossom?"

On "Peaseblossom", in a shower of spittle, the donkey dentures shot from Chris' mouth like a bar of soap from a hand in the bath, landed on the summit of his not inconsiderable paunch, chattered their way down and collapsed smiling and contented in his baggy corduroy crotch. For a second, open-mouthed astonishment from Chris and all on stage.

It's one of those seconds that lasts about an hour.

What was that?

And where did it land?

Chris can't see the donkey dentures over his stomach, but I and the audience and the other eight people on stage are transfixed by the grinning escapees resting between his legs.

A roar of laughter from the audience. Giggles on stage. Chris follows the stare of two thousand and eight pairs of eyes, locates the gremlin grin between his legs, and with great aplomb, palms them like a magician performing a card trick, wipes his hand across his face, and pops the slimy fuckers back into his mouth.

By now, the deliriously happy audience give the biggest round of the evening and with immense self control we try, and mostly succeed, to continue the play.

This week has gone incredibly quickly. I can't believe it's Saturday already. I'm beginning to have pangs of sadness at the thought of leaving Stratford.

I like it so much here. Helped no doubt by the golden light of an Indian summer, and blue skies blotted with occasional clouds that bring a gentle shower. Blissful Stratford upon Avon. As imagined and as remembered when a boy.

SEVENTEEN

When I walk around Stratford I can't pass the site of Shakespeare's house, New Place, without feeling a bubbling of anger in my gut that wants to erupt and have revenge in person on the Reverend Francis Gastrell. I have an unreasonable feeling of being cheated that I wasn't around in 1759, or he isn't around now, so that I could personally give him a good slapping for the malicious acts that secure the ecclesiastical old turd a small but devastating place in Stratford history.

This is what happened.

After his success in London, Shakespeare returned to Stratford and purchased from the Clopton family the second biggest house in the town. It was called New Place and from 1610 he lived there with his family for the last six years of his life.

When he died he left New Place to his daughter, Susanna, wife of the aforementioned Dr John Hall.

When she died, New Place was inherited by their daughter, Elizabeth Hall. On her death, it was passed back to the Clopton family. Later the Cloptons sold it to the Reverend Francis Gastrell.

I suspect he bought it for reasons other than the obvious attraction of a big house with a beautiful garden in the centre of town. Already by this time, the New Place property had become a shrine to the greatest poet that ever lived. People would come to Stratford to pay homage and to look at the mulberry tree planted in the garden of New Place by Shakespeare himself. The Reverend Fucking Ghastly didn't like people looking at his tree planted by the Bard of Avon.

So, did he build a wall or plant other trees to mask the mulberry tree?

Did he bollocks.

In 1756, the Reverend Fucking Ghastly, under divine guidance, or perhaps divine spite, cut the mulberry tree down.

Destroyed it. Not a trace. Dead. Gone.

Three years later in 1759, people were still arriving in Stratford to see New Place where the Bard lived and died. But the Reverend was not happy about this – so did he sell the property? Did he let it?

Did he bollocks.

This was a man of the cloth with a mission – perhaps a divine mission. So what did he do?

Are you ready for this?

He had New Place demolished.

Pulled it down until only the foundations remained.

The inhabitants of Stratford at the time were so incensed at the misguided procreant's malicious act that he was ostracised and driven out of town and settled in a neighbouring village to read his hate-mail.

Whenever I remember this story, my blood is fired to boiling. Shouldn't there be a ritual burning of his ghastly effigy annually in Stratford?

Forget Guy Fawkes, he failed.

This *Guy* succeeded, succeeded in depriving the nation, the world, of a glimpse, a small insight into the life of one of the most gifted men God, his God presumably, ever put on the planet.

Sentimental tosh? I don't think so.

Much of Shakespeare's work was considered diabolical by the church for many years, and the destruction of his habitat yet another blot in the book of good deeds wrought through the hypocritical fervour of religious zeal. Why is religion never the first and always the last to catch up with what is going on in the world?

EIGHTEEN

"If at first you don't succeed,
pack it in."

Eric Morecambe

In the afternoon a rehearsal for *The Faerie Queene*. Amanda Harris, Chris Benjamin, Ian Hughes and myself agreed about a month ago to do readings based around Spenser's poem *The Faerie Queene*, with orchestra playing music by Mendelssohn and Purcell in the RSC's Swan Theatre next Sunday. This is not an RSC project, it's a charity fund-raising event.

The goal of the evening, I'm told, is to raise money for the Rudolf Kempe Society in support of young musicians.

Cordula Kempe, widow of the conductor Rudolf, is organising the evening. She is a pleasant, middle-aged German Anglophile and an accomplished violinist. When not in Germany, she lives in Stratford, in one of the pretty little cottages adjacent to the Dirty Duck. The pretty little cottage parlour is where the rehearsal is held.

Her knowledge of music is formidable. Her organisational skills are less so, and it would seem, lack the Teutonic precision required at this point.

We're all a bit nervous about this enterprise as it now seems to be rather thrown together. At the first production meeting we're told we won't get a rehearsal with the orchestra until the day of performance. Some of the speeches have to tie in with the musical accompaniment in a fairly complicated way. Chris is the only one of us who reads music. Cordula seems to be under the illusion she can give us a cue, like a conductor to a section of an orchestra, and that we will magically play the notes, or in our case, say words to the notes. As we leave, I suggest to the cast that we must try and arrange some private rehearsals so we don't look like total prats on the night.

This is one of those ventures that one agrees to do and almost immediately a red light flashes accompanied by a warning voice that whispers,

"Are you sure this is a good idea? Even for charity?"

The red light is extinguished and the warning voice ignored by the actor's greed to perform. And there is temptation in the piece: a full orchestra, the music of Purcell and Mendelssohn, and the words of Spenser and Shakespeare, among others.

I offload some of my Spenser onto a willing Ian. It's written in Olde English but my now panicking, dyslexic vision sees it only in hieroglyphics.

There was far too much talk from Cordula of "winging it" for my taste. "Winging it" in my experience is far too frequently synonymous with – "egg on face".

The evenings are drawing in, the clocks went back on Saturday, the temperature has noticeably dropped a few degrees and I'm beginning to feel the need of warmer clothing. It's already getting dark by 4.30 pm as we leave the warmth and cosiness of Cordula's cottage and scurry along the cold, damp, black street to the theatre, then a snack and a rest in preparation for the evening's performance.

NINETEEN

In 1979 I was lucky enough to be asked to play Yasha in a production of *The Cherry Orchard* by Chekhov in a new adaptation by Peter Gill, who also directed.

It was the opening production of Riverside Studios in Hammersmith, London. A golden memory. A profoundly satisfying experience from the start of its six-week rehearsals to the finish of its limited six-week run. The cast – Judy Parfitt, Eleanor Bron, Julie Covington, Caroline Langrishe, Elizabeth Estensen, George Howe, Stephen Rea, David Pugh, Philip Locke, Ron Pember, Wensley Pithey, Michael Elphick and myself – had all agreed a salary of fifty quid a week. Why do the things one does for love so often turn out to be more rewarding than the money jobs? I hear it referred to still as a landmark production.

Rehearsing with Peter Gill is like being a privileged member of a masterclass. One exhilarating day after another as the play released its secrets, and the world of the big house with the beloved cherry orchard, and the people who inhabit it are revealed.

This became an auspicious journey for the cast at each and every celebrity-packed performance.

But for all the brouhaha that surrounded the theatre intelligentsia that lauded Peter's production, my most vivid memory is the last night.

In the last act, about 20 minutes from the end of the play, Lopakhin – played by Michael Elphick – enters with Yasha – played by me – carrying a bottle of champagne and glasses, which Lopakhin opens and places on a pile of trunks packed with the belongings of the departing family. Yasha sits morosely up stage on the trunks with his back to the audience and drinks the entire bottle of champagne – a mock-up prop of ginger ale – whilst the goodbye scene is taking place downstage. He has about ten minutes to down the contents of the bottle in time for Lopakhin to announce –

"There's champagne here suitable for the occasion"

– notice the bottle is empty, tip it upside down and, with an accusatory look at Yasha, say –

"But somebody's drunk the lot."

I've detested ginger ale ever since: merely a sip now gives me a taste memory of downing a pint of the revolting stuff each performance and the resulting acid indigestion throughout the rest of the night.

I didn't have this particular problem after performance on the last night because Mike Elphick had a cure for my acid indigestion by switching the prop bottle of ginger ale for a pukka French bottle of the real thing. The challenging glint in his eye as he popped the cork on stage and the pungent smell of the real alcohol told me I was up shit creek without a paddle.

You may know there's a theatrical tradition of pulling pranks on each other on a last night. Letters and notes delivered on stage usually contain jokes or obscenities on such occasions. In the worst scenario this sudden shock can, and has been known to, produce uncontrollable hysterical snorts, guffaws of laughter, spittle and snot, rendering the actor unable to deliver his or her next line. In the best scenario you manage to proceed as if nothing has happened and plan how to get your own back in the next scene.

Finding a live goldfish that Timothy Dalton had put in my communion cup whilst playing a priest in *The Royal Hunt of the Sun* as a young actor in Rep is one that springs to mind.

I sit on the trunks with the bottle of champagne in my hand reluctantly admiring this one, clever and daring. Other than wimping out, I have no choice other than to finish the bottle.

In ten minutes, the bottle is empty.

I can see Mike is impressed when he approaches, tips the bottle upside down and says with true astonishment –

"But somebody's drunk the lot."

I'm pleased with my accomplishment – well I'm pleased with just about everything. With supreme self-control I oscillate my way through the last few minutes of the play, and at the curtain as we stand next to each other and take our bow, Mike whispers a gravelly congratulations.

"Well done son."

"You bashtard," I reply.

Games of this sort sometimes serve a higher purpose. As a result of this performance, seen by the influential casting director Mary Selway, who was in the audience, I was cast to play Alec D'Urberville in Roman Polanski's film *Tess*. No interview, no film tests, no meetings, a straight offer with a script, and ten glorious months in France playing a major role in a classic film I'm very proud of.

Thanks Mike.

Today I went to see a matinee performance of *The Cherry Orchard* directed by Adrian Noble in the Swan Theatre. It was the same Peter Gill adaptation we did that happy time ago at Riverside Studios. This afternoon was an extraordinary experience, inspired and inspiring, focused and precise in its storytelling, acting and direction. A true ensemble piece as it must be, as all great theatre must be.

It made me laugh, it made me cry, a trickle of a tear in the first act, by the end of the play a fistful of soggy Kleenex.

When Lopakhin, superbly played by David Troughton, is struggling to propose marriage to Varya, a heartbreaking performance by Kate Duchene, Lopakhin holds her hand an interminable length of time but the words just won't come out and you want to scream "Ask her, for God's sake say it", but he can't, and you know both their hopes of ever finding happiness lie in shatters.

Towards the end of the play Alec McCowen, playing Gayev, gazes out front to his beloved cherry orchard, as he is about to leave for the last time; he says nothing, but the pain, the regret, the sadness, and disappointment in his eyes say it all. He then throws himself onto Ranyevskaya's shoulder and cries,

"Sister, my sister."

That breaks your heart.

This afternoon was full of such transporting moments. The actors took the play away from the author, away from the director, and in the wooden "O" of the magical Swan Theatre, gave us a glimpse through a floating bubble of the world they inhabited.

I was grateful for a time to recover from this experience before having to go on for our evening performance.

The Cherry Orchard finished at 4.15 pm. Into the theatre wigs and hair department at 4.30 pm for a beard dye.

5.30 pm – 6.30 pm: A private rehearsal with Chris, Ian and Amanda for *The Faerie Queene* that we do this Sunday in the Swan Theatre.

6.45 pm – 7 pm: A neck and shoulder massage.

7.30 pm: Curtain up. Do the show.

10.45 pm: To the Dirty Duck for a Halloween party for the company arranged by landlady Pam Harris. A short while later the public are asked to drink up and when the last one is ushered out, we are served sausages in soft bread rolls with chips and tomato ketchup, and pints of beer. A competition for the best cut-out Halloween pumpkin was declared a draw by Pam, and all contestants won a bottle of champagne.

Some of *The Cherry Orchard* company were present and we exchange stories, compare notes, tell jokes, swap anecdotes. An extremely useful time: opinions are given and taken freely, usually kindly, but always with a passion, born of a company with one common objective. Whether the excellence sought is achieved is a matter of opinion, but it is sought and that makes my heart sing.

I realise yet again we've spent the entire evening talking about theatre, writers, actors, directors, music. The enthusiasm is quite extraordinary and for me the most congenial company to be in. Floated home through the churchyard, not a ghosty ghouly stirred.

    2.30 am To bed with Vivaldi and a heart that sings.

TWENTY

Still worried about this one, spoken to Puck whilst Titania lies
sleeping in her bower with Bottom.

OBERON: "Seest thou this sweet sight?
    Her dotage now I do being to pity;
    For, meeting her of late behind the wood
    Seeking sweet favour for this hateful fool,
    I did upbraid her and fall out with her,
    For she his hairy temples then had rounded
    With coronet of fresh and fragrant flowers;
    And that same dew, which sometime on the buds
    Was wont to swell like round and orient pearls,
    Stood now within the pretty flowerets' eyes
    Like tears that did their own disgrace bewail.
    When I had at my pleasure taunted her,
    And she in mild terms begged my patience,
    I then did ask of her her changeling child,
    Which straight she gave me, and her fairy sent
    To bear him to my bower in Fairyland.
    And now I have the boy, I will undo
    This hateful imperfection in her eyes.
    And, gentle Puck, take the transformed scalp
    From off the head of this Athenian swain,
    That, he awaking when the other do,
    May all to Athens back again repair,
    And think no more of this night's accidents
    But as the fierce vexation of a dream.
    But first I will release the Fairy Queen.
    Be as thou wast wont to be;
    See as thou wast wont to see;
    Dian's bud o'er Cupid's flower
    Hath such force and blessed power.
    Now, my Titania, wake you, my sweet Queen!"

It's a lot of information, elegantly crammed into 30 lines, but it's just feeling like exposition – which of course is exactly what it is, albeit dressed up with dew and flowerets, bugs and petals. It's the last of my major stumbling blocks. I worry still about serving the poetry fully. I think I'm complicating the speech. I want to try a much simpler line. I think in the past I've maybe worked it too hard. It's the classic Shakespeare monologue form. State problem – analyse problem – reach resolution.

Of course, the man himself said it all in Hamlet's advice to the player.

> HAMLET: "Speak the speech, I pray you, as I pronounced it to you, trippingly on the tongue. But if you mouth it, as many of our players do, I had as lief the town crier spoke my lines. Nor do not saw the air too much with your hand, thus, but use all gently, for in the very torrent, tempest, and (as I may say) whirlwind of your passion, you must acquire and beget a temperance that may give it smoothness. O, it offends me to the soul to hear a robustious periwig-pated fellow tear a passion to tatters, to very rags, to split the ears of the ground-lings, who for the most part are capable of nothing but inexplicable dumb shows and noise I would have such a fellow whipped for o'erdoing Termagant. It out-herods Herod. Pray you avoid it.
>
> "Be not too tame neither, but let your own discretion be your tutor. Suit the action to the word, the word to the action, with this special observance, that you o'erstep not the modesty of nature. For anything so o'erdone is from the purpose of playing, whose end, both at the first and now, was and is, to hold, as 'twere, the mirror up to nature; to show virtue her own feature, scorn her own image, and the very age and body of the time his form and pres-

sure. Now, this o'erdone, or come tardy off, though it makes the unskilful laugh, cannot but make the judicious grieve, the censure of which one must in your allowance o'erweigh a whole theatre of others. O, there be players that I have seen play, and heard others praise, and that highly (not to speak it profanely), that neither having th'accent of Christians, nor the gait of Christian, pagan, nor man, have so strutted and bellowed that I have thought some of Nature's journeymen had made men, and not made them well, they imitated humanity so abominably."

Question – So why is the above so fucking difficult?
Answer – If it was easy everyone would be doing it.

I was very grateful, and not a little relieved, to be told tonight by a couple of ladies waiting at the stage door after the show, that, having seen other productions of *The Dream* before, this was the first time they had truly understood Theseus' kindness in his speech in defence of watching Bottom and his gang do their play. This chance meeting at the stage door gave me a disproportionate amount of much-needed confidence that what I was trying to do was at least working for some.

 THESEUS: "The kinder we, to give them thanks for nothing.
  Our sport shall be to take what they mistake;
  And what poor duty cannot do, noble respect
  Takes it in might, not merit.
  Where I have come, great clerks have purposed
  To greet me with premeditated welcomes,
  Where I have seen them shiver and look pale,
  Make periods in the midst of sentences,
  Throttle their practised accent in their fears,
  And in conclusion dumbly have broke off,
  Not paying me a welcome. Trust me, sweet,

Out of this silence yet I picked a welcome,
And in the modesty of fearful duty
I read as much as from the rattling tongue
Of saucy and audacious eloquence.
Love, therefore, and tongue-tied simplicity
In least speak most, to my capacity."

Acting is about choices. So much depends on the confidence one has in those choices. But with a sure grip on the handle, the doors are opened to all manner of possibilities that suddenly take place.

TWENTY-ONE

Twiggs has arrived. Her welcome smile, hug and kiss light up my life. And I need a flashlight at the moment. I can't see my way into giving this evening's performance of *The Faerie Queene* without it.

My concern was in no way alleviated when, with considerable trepidation, I arrived at Cordula Kempe's cottage for the morning rehearsal. She greets me at the door making a supreme effort to be her usual polite self, but cannot disguise the panic in her voice, and yes, fear in her eyes. It's evident from her erratic hyper-active behaviour and the alarming amount of perspiration dripping from her chin, nose and upper lip that this is not due to the central heating, but that the lady is with agonising self-control managing to just about stay this side of panic. I became genuinely concerned for her health, and found myself formulating a plan of action if and when she had a seizure.

Within 20 minutes of rehearsal I realise any small hope I had that "winging it" can bring any advantage at all, does indeed wing it – out of the open latticed window – and evaporates in the thin autumn air, pursued by Mendelssohn's notes from the piano. I wish I could join them.

Any dream of an auspicious debut in the Swan Theatre has every chance of remaining just that – a dream.

We manage to mark through some of the music cues. At 2 pm we break for a bite to eat before assembling in the theatre with the orchestra at 2.30 pm.

Chaos ensues.

We find we have two and a half hours to rehearse a three-hour show.

Twenty minutes into rehearsal it's discovered the string section of the orchestra has different music to the wind section. The soprano and the actors sit in a semi-circle in front of the orchestra. Cordula on lead violin sits directly behind my chair. The conductor grows increasingly irate, nurtured in his frustration by a continuous effort on Cordula's part to take over his role.

Eventually, he explodes.

"If you think you can do it better, here, take the baton."

He points the baton at her. I have no doubt, had his baton been a poisoned dart, Cordula would have been put out of her agony. As would we all.

"I told you two and a half weeks ago that an hour of the show should have been cut, but you refused," he hurls at Cordula.

Panic, panic, panic. Panic rules OK. Panic from the orchestra. Panic from the soprano. Panic from the actors.

Panic from Cordula, who like a visionless clairvoyant replies, with no conviction at all:

"It'll be all right tonight."

Pointing his baton like the poisoned dart he wished it was, the conductor speaks for us all.

"No it won't be all right tonight. If it isn't all right now it won't be all right when we come to do it before the public."

We slog on.

By the end of rehearsal we're only halfway through the piece. The soprano still hasn't rehearsed three of her songs, the conductor hasn't had time to work out his cues, the actors don't know when to speak, the orchestra are concerned whether they all have the same music for the second half.

Cordula is a robot at the point of self-destruct, wandering amongst the orchestra and performers like an automaton, repeating her mantra –

"It'll be all right tonight."

"It'll be all right tonight."

I'm not comfortable with "all right". It's not a goal I'm familiar with or in my opinion worthy of pursuit.

Ian is distressed because only about 100 tickets have been sold. I'm relieved. The fewer people witnessing the inevitable humiliation the better.

By the evening, however, the house is surprisingly full.

Ian speaks first –

"Enter Hippolyta, Theseus and winded trumpets sound."

Amanda and I stand and step forward.

"Not yet," yells out Cordula in a voice perfectly audible to the entire gathering.

Amanda and I return to our Teutonic seats and Cordula, without missing a bow beat, plays for another two or three minutes at the end of which she shouts –

"Now."

The audience giggle, and Ian declares –

"Theseus and Hippolyta enter again, and again winded trumpets sound."

Amanda and I stand again and again step forward.

We recite a long passage of exposition, where for some reason very slow dirgy pieces of music have been set, making every word uttered sound like the last rites. This piece dutifully dies a death.

There was much twinkling in the actors' eyes, flashing thespodic morse, one to another.

"This doesn't work –"

"I know, let's just keep going, perhaps it will get better –"

"Not getting any better, is it? –"

"No –"

"Help, don't know what the fuck happens next –"

"Don't look at me, I haven't got a clue. Or cue –"

"Don't you wish you weren't here? –"

"I'd rather be in Trinity churchyard. Dead –"

"Oh my God, she's shouting out again, pretend not to hear –"

"Can't pretend, the audience are laughing –"

"Best join in the fun –"

But the adrenaline kicks in, professional pride intervenes. Between us we manage to pull something out of the ragbag of disarray. At moments the beauty of the music and the sung or spoken word transcend our unpreparedness and the audible prompting, tutting and blowing from the Teutonic lady on lead violin behind me.

There were moments where we seemed able to, yes, "wing it". A bit of improvisation and messing about, some fun things emerged.

Kind people said it was a most enjoyable evening. Honest people stayed schtumm.

There were drinks back at Cordula's after the show. Although quite what she was celebrating I couldn't grasp. Getting through the day without a coronary? Thirty musicians and actors getting through the day without a coronary?

Twiggs and I slipped away to enjoy dinner à deux at Lambs restaurant which seems to be the only restaurant in Stratford open at 10.30 pm on a Sunday.

A discovery that made the endeavour almost worthwhile tonight was this little gem, which I so enjoyed reciting:

What Is It?

"It is madness says Reason. It is what it is, says Love,
   It is unhappiness, says Caution, It is nothing but pain,
      says Fear,
   It has no future, says Insight. It is what it is, says Love,
   It is ridiculous, says Pride, It is foolish, says Caution,
   It is impossible, says Experience, It is what it is, says
      Love."

Eric Freid

TWENTY-TWO

> "I've had a perfectly wonderful
> evening. But this wasn't it."
> *Groucho Marx*

A rare dreadful evening doing *The Dream* tonight, really depressing and discouraging.

A lack of enthusiasm from the audience, very little reaction or at least very little compared to what we have become accustomed to. Not only my experience, many of the cast came off stage looking and feeling as if they'd just had their earlobe bitten off by Mike Tyson.

"No such thing as a bad house, only a bad performance." I've heard said. Well bollocks, this was a crap house, we ran ourselves ragged for them. I think they, and certainly we, wished we'd all stayed home to watch telly.

A surprisingly warm reception at the end even so. So what do I know?

To the Greek Connection restaurant after the show. Twiggs and I sat quietly in a corner of the crowded restaurant. Spirits lifted at the end of the evening by some customers throwing themselves drunkenly and passionately into the handkerchief-holding twists and turns of Zorba-type dances, and the smashing of a few dozen plates.

On the way home, we pass a newsagent's shop window displaying my wife's picture on the cover of a couple of magazines; I turn to look at her, and she smiles me a magazine cover.

November 5th – Guy Fawkes Night. A few minutes before the show this evening, I stand on my dressing room balcony overlooking the river ready to go on stage in make-up, gold brocade tunic, gold harem pants, gold shoes, voluminous gold cloak.

I just about fit in the tiny space. When I do, I dim the watery moon.

Two hundred yards to my left stands the old stone bridge with its cavernous arches reflected in the water like eight enormous black mouths drinking the river. Quiet. Peaceful.

Suddenly a terrifying barrage of explosions as if the order "Let Battle Commence" has been silently signalled.

Smoke and flashing lights from behind the bridge, rockets and roman candles climb whirring, whizzing, whining into the night sky. Formations of fiery reds, golds, blues and greens segue high above the bridge and implode into bright peacock tails that fold into a cascade of falling stars. Red Hot Pokers zoom menacingly across the river like enemy gunfire and pop and fizz into its waters. Rockets soar like Exocet missiles. Jumping Jacks and Bangers, unseen but alarmingly loud, pierce the night's dull ear.

Then an extraordinary sight. Swans, geese, ducks, moorhens, wrens, every species of feathered creature living on the river, burst through or over the gaping mouths of the bridge, towards me like a naval convoy with air support. Fierce and fearful swans and geese at full kilter flap frantic cackling like machine guns, ducks paddle panicked and honk a foghorn warning, Dive, Dive, Dive. The night river is littered with frigates, battleships, destroyers and cruisers. Feathery craft of every size and description scrambling for safety, scuttling to make it home. It's Dunkirk.

What am I witnessing? Who am I? Am I in a dream? Is it real or in the play? Am I Oberon or me?

PUCK: "And forth my mimic comes. When they him spy –
    As wild geese that the creeping fouler eye,
    Or russet-pated choughs, many in sought
    Rising and cawing at the guns report,
    Sever themselves and madly sweep the sky –
    So at his sight away his fellows fly."

Standing on the balcony like a spectre looking over the surreal display, I feel a surge of childish omnipotent power.

I'm in charge of all I survey. I created it. And with a sweep of my golden cloak I have the power to change it, wipe all before me away and create another scene at will.

The spell is quickly broken by the stage manager's announcement over the dressing room speaker.

"Beginners please, this is your Beginners call. Miss Harris, Mr Lawson, Mr Hughes, on stage please, this is your Beginners call."

Ian and I stand in the wings waiting to go on.

"What are you smiling at?" he asks.

"Me? Oh, I'm just remembering a story I heard once about a young boy at school who when asked by his teacher what he wanted to be when he grew up replied,

"'Please miss, I'd like to be an actor when I grow up miss',

"And the teacher says to the boy,

"'Well dear, you can't do both'."

Throughout the evening's show, the muffled bangs and whoops of war continue outside but far from intruding they somehow enhance the strange happenings on stage. For me, anyway. A flash of the recent experience on my dressing-room balcony bizarrely enhances the imagery of:

OBERON: "My gentle Puck, come hither. Thou rememberest
    Since once I sat upon a promontory,
    And heard a mermaid on a dolphin's back
    Uttering such dulcet and harmonious breath
    That the rude sea grew civil at her song,
    And certain stars shot madly from their spheres
    To hear the sea-maid's music?"

PUCK: "I remember."

OBERON: "That very time I saw (but thou coulds't not)
    Flying between the cold moon and the earth
    Cupid all armed: a certain aim he took
    At a fair vestal thronèd by the west,

And loosed his loveshaft smartly from his bow
As it should pierce a hundred thousand hearts;
But I might see young Cupid's fiery shaft
Quenched in the chaste beams of the watery moon."

For all that we were presented with an audience tonight very similar to last night's. Two dodos in succession. We've been spoiled, and last night we were taken by surprise. The lack of participation from the audience wrong-footed us, we lost our rhythms, became unsure, tentative, overcompensated, forgot a golden rule – never whore yourself to the audience.

But not tonight. Tonight we spotted it immediately and a quick regrouping took place backstage after the first scene.

We decided to up the stakes, increase the energy by a few thousand volts, give them ECT. Don't allow them to be a lazy audience.

Managed to have a quickly-grabbed word backstage with the four young lovers who are concerned by the lack of response. As in war, theatre tradition embraces the convention that the older, more experienced campaigner might be worth listening to at such times.

I suggest:

"Don't pander to them, don't let them dictate the pace, make them come to us, let them know if they want a fun night they have to keep up with us – we're not waiting, the train is leaving the station, you'd better get on board if you want to join us for the journey."

Halfway through the first Oberon scene, I begin to feel the audience coming towards us. By interval time we're clearly winning, they're coming with us. By the end of the show, they're ours.

A sense of achievement this evening in winning this audience over. It was a rough ride. The vampires sucked us dry.

A quick pit stop at the Dirty Duck.

Through the churchyard home. I was told today many suicides have taken place in this churchyard. Actors in despair after audiences like our last two?

A cruel damp east wind prevails, buffeting the trees, lifting and swirling the skeletal leaves causing them to dance like demons on the ancient graves –

> PUCK: "Now it is the time of night
>   That the graves, all gaping wide,
>   Every one lets forth its sprite,
>   In the churchway paths to glide."

Was he remembering the path I am now treading when he wrote these lines? I stop at the church door.

"Were you?" I ask.

Another ghostly gush of sharp unfriendly wind sets leaves whirling like spectres, telling me to go home.

I'm not welcome here tonight.

> "Oh lost, and by the wind grieved,
>   Ghost come back again."

*

> "Some cause happiness wherever
>   they go. Others, whenever
>   they go."
>
> *Oscar Wilde*

Oh God help us. Two more depressingly frustrating erratic shows, as far as the cast were concerned anyway. Now I've mostly enjoyed playing to our occasional school audiences. But this afternoon's matinee demanded adjustments of a new and different dimension. A mob of over-excited teenagers. The shouting, whooping and whistling before and during the first half of the play from the undisciplined pubescents should have shamed the accompanying teachers supposedly in charge. They were not here to listen and soak up some Shakespeare – they were here to take the piss.

I was so incensed at their behaviour right from the start, and so acutely aware of the sprinkling of regular theatregoers present by their repeated shushes and pleas for quiet, that when I explain to Hermia the only choices she has if she refuses to marry Demetrius are:

> "Either to die the death or to abjure
> Forever the society of men,"

I opened my mouth tonight and out came:

> "Either to die the death or to *enjoy*
> Forever the society of men."

Not quite what the author had in mind.

In the interval, Chris Benjamin says, "We're playing to a house full of yobs."

Before the start of Act Two more unruly aggressive whooping, stamping, shouting and whistling – confirming the feeling that this is more a celebration of getting an afternoon off school than a celebration of an afternoon at the theatre.

I enter, take my position centre stage as the lights go up. I stand in silent defiance maybe a minute, maybe two, and let them know I'm not starting until they shut the fuck up. Now there's a difference. I know enthusiasm when I hear it. Chris was right, this was a bunch of yobs – taking the piss.

After the show, two of the teachers from different schools, supposedly in charge, stood yelling at each other across the emptying auditorium, having a stand-up row, each accusing the other of being responsible for the disgraceful behaviour of their charges, seemingly unaware they were setting the very example that their pupils had been emulating. The teenagers, not surprisingly, looked on with glee.

The evening show was dull. Full, but dull.

An unnerving experience. But these audiences in their varying ways are unnerving.

It's hard to find rhythm to play to. Physically and mentally draining. I asked our assistant director if he would drop by my dressing room for a chat. I've become increasingly concerned over the last few days about one or two aspects of the show that are beginning to emerge due to the type of audiences we've been playing to.

There's the beginning of a fear in me that we are pandering to their tastes, rather than the other way round. A danger of parts of the play becoming coarsened in an attempt to court the audience's favour. He agrees. This can happen quite easily and subconsciously and in very small and subtle ways. But the structure and integrity of this production just can't sustain that, and must at all costs be preserved. Previously, we've experienced occasions when the audience and players are so at one you feel you're almost breathing in time with each other.

Not so this afternoon. Not so tonight. Not so for the last few performances. Us or them?

Hard to define. I want to think it's them. But why? It's been happening for the last few performances, so it could be us. What are we doing wrong?

Another problem. These last few audiences seem to be mostly appreciating the physical and visual side of the show, but are not really getting into the text. And we're not getting the reactions to our lines that, as players, we like and need to get.

Sitting atop my red door with a bird's-eye view of the young lovers' scene, each performance is still a total joy.

Tonight for a mind-blowing moment we all freeze into a frieze.

Become at once a pattern on a Greek vase. A Zoffany drawing. The small figures in a 17th-century illustration of the

Globe Theatre. The pictures on the walls you see at the Garrick Club.

An overwhelming feeling of continuity. Continuity.

Should have gone to The Duck and got drunk after two shows from hell, but glad I didn't. Walking home through the church-yard, I see ahead of me a tall, thin, slightly bowed silhouette of a man.

I quicken my pace to catch the figure up. I introduce myself.

Peter Copley is in his eighties, he's playing Firs in *The Cherry Orchard*. I express my appreciation for the production and his performance as we walk together to Havenside.

"Thank you." He graciously says. "I saw you in *The Dream* last week."

I thank the gods it wasn't this week.

"I thought it was marvellous," he continued. "I didn't have time to come round and I'm a bit old for all those stairs now, you know. You played Yasha in Peter Gill's original adaptation, didn't you?"

"Yes, that's right, nearly 20 years ago."

"I played Yasha 60 years ago. I remember it as if it were yesterday," the old man said.

And there it was again. Greek vase. Zoffany drawing. Clap. Whistle. Stamp. Shout. Cheers. Silence. Continuity.

For a moment walking together, I'm him in the future. He's me in the past.

TWENTY-THREE

A rainbow has just appeared outside the window of my flat at Havenside. Arcing over head and down over the river into the pine trees opposite, the primary colours are astonishingly vivid. It is the brightest, most magnificent, picture-book-perfect rainbow I've witnessed since I was a child; the enamelled colours remind me of the palette used for our play.

I'm tempted to try to cross the river and go into the copse to see if I can find the pot of gold. Perhaps I've already found it. Maybe this is my pot of gold.

As the clouds begin to recede, and a blue sky breaks through the scarf of slate clouds, so the rainbow begins to fade. For a long moment all that is left is a luminous column of red, orange, yellow, gold, green, blue, indigo and violet, rising like a Disney-land monolith from the cluster of pines on the far bank of the river. There's a flock of geese, silent silvettes flying across the river towards the rainbow.

God, it is beautiful here, at the end of the rainbow. Magical.

A phenomenon. I discover it's not a pot of gold at the end of the rainbow. It's two.

I clutch the telephone to my ear. It's Sybil Burton and Emma Walton ringing from the Bay Street Theatre, New York, where I did *Two Keys* two lifetimes ago. They say they would like us to open the season after next with *Noël and Gertie*. The piece I gave to Sybil to read on my last night in Sag Harbor. Twiggy playing Gertrude Lawrence, me directing.

Over a year away. But it's a promise.

So what's a year?

Well in my experience a year is a catastrophic twelve months in your life never to be forgotten, or alternatively a happy 52 weeks you can hardly remember.

I am cognisant of this as I open the suitcase of books I have with me, including a Noël Coward autobiography, his diaries, a volume of his plays – and this is only a small part of my collection. Did this man never stop writing? A library, eventually, to read through, but I intend to read every word. Dozens of songs to listen to, but I intend to listen to every note of every Coward song ever written. I've got time.

I ring Tony Walton in New York. My *Two Keys* director and the best set and costume designer in the world. Also the nicest man on the planet. I love Tony, he loves me, I love his wife, he loves mine, he loves my children, I love his, I want him to design our sets and costumes. He can't say no.

But he does. Says he is, as usual, incredibly busy. I plead. Say I can't do it without him. And in truth I can't. Tony is also a Coward aficionado – what he doesn't know about Coward ain't worth knowing.

I beg: "It's over a year away Tony, please try and find us a little corner at your table."

He says he will have to look at things and see what he can do. I take this as a definite yes.

Things could still go wrong. It's a year away. But I have a warm feeling about this one. Something tells me it's going to happen. I need to keep all of this under my hat, but I also have to live with the argumentative Oberon and Theseus, who I am afraid just don't get on at all. Now William and Noël are also moving in together, who thank God I can't help feeling somehow will get on much better. When my head hits my pillow I see them happily in the parlour together – Noël at piano – doing a duet, with Will speaking his words and Noël singing his song "You Were There":

> "Tomorrow and Tomorrow and Tomorrow
> *Was it in the real world*
> Creeps in this petty pace from day to day
> *Or was it in a dream,*
> Till the last syllable of recorded time
> *Or was it just a note from some eternal theme.*

And all our yesterdays have lighted fools, the way to
  dusky death.
Was it accidental or accurately planned?
Out, out brief candle, life's but a walking shadow
How could I hesitate
Knowing that my fate
Held me by the hand?
A poor player that struts and frets his hour upon the
  stage
You were there, I met you and my heart stopped beating
And then is heard no more.
You were there and in that first enchanted meeting
Life changed its tune
The stars, the moon
Came near to me
Dreams that I dreamed
Like magic seemed
To be clear to me, dear to me.
It is a tale told by an idiot
You were there
Your eyes looked into mine and faltered
Everywhere
The colour of the whole world altered
Full of sound and fury
False became true, my universe tumbled into,
The earth became heaven, for you
Signifying nothing
Were there."

And so on until sleep rescues me.

Thank you, God, Twiggs has arrived and was part of an
absolutely remarkable audience tonight. With us every twist
and turn. Hoots of delight, sometimes two or three rounds of

applause within the space of a few minutes. We just sailed along together. It was bliss.

An ever-intriguing mystery how one night the same part of a show can be greeted with delight and spontaneous rounds of applause, and with another house get hardly a giggle.

And you can never second-guess, until the curtain goes up, which it's going to be. A joyous evening. No gremlins.

After this happy experience a walk with the Missus over Clopton's bridge to David Troughton's house for another. An end-of-run party for both companies, *The Orchard* cast and *The Dream* team, also some welcome faces from the Barbican in London who are up to see friends in the company. Fireworks and sparklers in the garden, a lot of vodka is being drunk, I stick to wine and the best spare ribs I've ever tasted in my life.

On occasions such as this, one can't help feeling a sense of family, of belonging, of, yes, my current obsession: Continuity.

It doesn't need, somehow indeed would be inappropriate, to voice what I am feeling tonight, perhaps what most are feeling.

The clamour of excitement in the air is tinged with a sadness. In a couple of days our time at Stratford is over. *The Cherry Orchard* goes to London, and we start our tour at the RSC's third home in Newcastle. Another circle. Newcastle is where I started rehearsals for *The Relapse* all those lifetimes ago when I began this story. But Stratford is where it must end. Newcastle, Plymouth, Japan, Hong Kong, New Zealand, Australia can surely not top this. Or can they? That's a wonderfully terrifying thought, but too big to contemplate when at about 2.30 am we walk back home over Clopton's awesome bridge, pungent, musky aroma from the river as we pass over the ancient stones. Along Waterside, past the theatre dark and dead as a mausoleum. Through Trinity churchyard, quiet and still tonight, a trace of burning wood in the damp night air.

At Havenside a glass of wine and a chat about the present and the future. We plan. God laughs. Eventually we realise it's 4 am and tumble into bed.

A lot of fragile-looking people wandering zombie-like around the theatre today. Apparently the party carried on till dawn.

I bump into a pale David Troughton and tell him he has a lot to answer for. One actor swears he doesn't remember anything, reckons he must have fallen over because his ribs are very bruised. He was trying to find out who the person was to thank who he vaguely remembers getting him home and putting him to bed. Hope he hasn't forgotten anything else!

Great show again tonight. Audience and us back to normal.

Dinner at Lambs after the show with Kathryn Hunter and Marcello Magni of the Theatre de Complicite who are co-directing *Everyman* at The Other Place, the RSC's studio theatre.

I first met them when we were all working in Clywd last year. I've loved Kathryn's work since first thrilling to her performance in the Complicite production of *The Three Lives of Lucy Cabrol* at Riverside Studios a few years ago. She has a remarkable and unique talent. Marcello is a gifted actor and director who brings mime and Commedia dell'Arte influences to his work. Kathryn quizzed me about Adrian Noble and Peter Hall's approach to speaking Shakespeare. I explained as best I could, but I fear it all sounds rather academic and dry in explanation over a dinner plate, it's only when you're up there it gets sexy.

Dreading the morrow and saying goodbye to Stratford.

TWENTY-FOUR

"Past and to come, seems best:
Things present worse."
                                        William Shakespeare

Last night in Stratford upon Avon. I awake with a leaden heart but determined to try and make this final performance at Stratford a meaningful occasion for Oberon, and Theseus, and me.

On the list today, to brave a new take on:

"I know a bank where the wild thyme blows..."

I don't know exactly what is going to change, it's more a feeling, a gut thing, a desire. This is one of Oberon's most famous arias, familiar to a good percentage of the audience, and to most of the ghosts hanging around in the wings. My job is to make them hear it for the first time.

Words are thoughts in the air: my friend Oberon grabbed those thoughts tonight, and as a result the first part of the outpour became suffused with longing, yearning and desire, a nostalgia for times past. Until, with anger that she should vitiate their love, the vitriol of the last few lines enrages and surprises even Oberon himself.

"...and with the juice of this I'll streak her eyes,
and make her full of hateful fantasies."

One discovery propels him to another until like a marathon runner something else takes over. Striding, strong. The text like a road beneath his feet. The exhilaration of the run as gratifying as the glory of the finishing line.

And then the final Stratford curtain.

Undone. Unmanned. I struggle to hold back the tears. No good. Everything blurs.

And it's over.

The sadness of goodbyes. After the show we put out a message over the dressing room loudspeakers to say goodbye to *The Cherry Orchard* cast, wishing them good luck in London, and thanking them for some happy hangovers. They reciprocate with a message wishing us luck on the tour and say how much they are going to miss seeing so many fairies in the wings of the theatre.

I remove my first night cards and telegrams from the walls of my dressing room – tradition dictates unlucky to do so before the final curtain. Pack my make-up and a few belongings. A last moment on the tiny balcony. Tomorrow dressing room 1A will belong to someone else. Continuity.

Say goodbye to Trinity Church, to Himself lying within.

At Havenside put two reluctant kittens in their carry-cage. Load the car with our belongings. I'm going to miss the laughing of the ducks and the call of the geese, the majesty of the swans and the sweet flowing Avon. Tomorrow the flat will be another actor's home. Continuity.

Can it all carry on as if I'd never been here when tomorrow dawns a new Stratford day? I suppose it must. It will miss me less than the void I feel in saying goodbye. Maybe the ancient town didn't even notice the local boy had been back for a brief while.

As we leave the town, I stop at the old red pillar box on the corner of Scholar's Lane to post a signed photograph to the Dirty Duck for the Actor's Wall.

Could the red lips be smiling as they swallow my envelope?

*

"Our names are written in water"
David Garrick

London 2.30 am. It's dark, but a little light seeps through a crack in the velvet curtains. I'm lying in bed, my wife beside me. I sneak out of bed, cross the room and close the doors. No visitors allowed.

Not Loveless. Not Hugo; not Vernon. Not Oberon; not Theseus. Not William; not Noël. Just me. And my dream.

"How true is that philosophy which says
Our heaven is seated in our minds!
Through all the roving pleasures of my youth,
Where nights and days seemed all consumed in joy,
Where the false face of luxury
Displayed such charms
As might have shaken the most holy hermit
And made him totter at his altar,
I never knew one moment's peace like this.
Here, in this little soft retreat,
My thoughts unbent from all the cares of life,
Content with fortune,
Eased from the grating duties of dependence,
From envy flee, ambition underfoot,
The raging flame of wild destructive lust
Reduced to a warm pleasing fire of lawful love,
My life glides on, and all is well within."

"What's past is prologue"
William Shakespeare

THE END